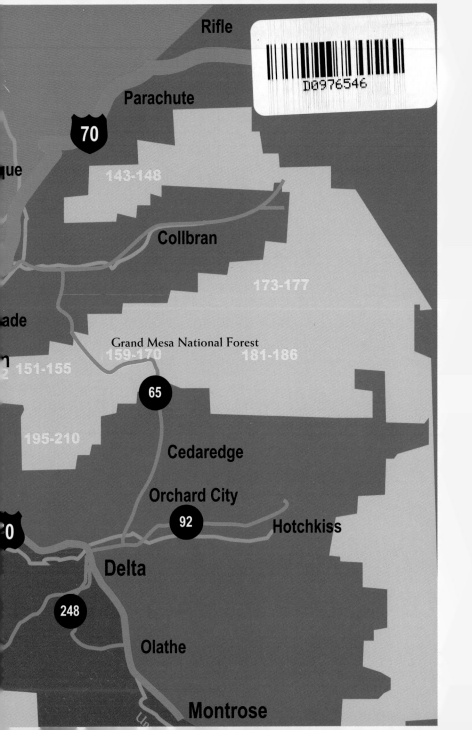

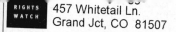

Copyright 2002 Nattana Johnson and Christopher Schnittker

CREDITS
Design and Production: Monument Graphics & Communications
Editors: Karen Shaw, Phillip Benningfield
Maps: Maptech

First edition.

ISBN 0-9714560-0-3

Letter from the editors:
Most of our lives we have spent exploring the land we live in. After recently moving to Grand Junction and discovering the lack of Grand Valley area trail information, we felt it was a great opportunity to create an area specific book—for all ages and human powered outdoor activities.

We have been pleasantly surprised and delighted at the Grand Valley area offerings. There are the crystalline lakes, dense lodgepole pine forests and boulder fields on the Grand Mesa. Arches and extraordinary rock formations parade throughout the Colorado National Monument, and wild horses romp behind the Book Cliffs while the Gunnison and Colorado rivers carve snaking grandiose canyons. All of this offers limitless exploration and includes some of the most diverse backcountry landscapes we have ever been exposed to. We are thrilled to present this guide, and hope you will find numerous days filled with remarkable outdoor endeavors.

We have tried hard to make this book error free. If you find any errors, please let us know. Email comments to bookinfo@OutdoorGuru.com

A Special thanks to our sponsors and advertisers
As you use this book and discover that you can't leave home without it, remember that the businesses listed here helped make it possible. Please support them as they have supported us.

SPONSORS
ADAM'S MARK HOTEL
BICYCLE OUTFITTERS
COUNTRY JAM
FRUITA REALTY
LANDROVER ROARING FORK
MONUMENT GRAPHICS
RUNNING OUTFITTERS

Bank of Grand Junction
Blue Moon Bar and Grille
Board & Buckle
Bocaza Mexican Grille
Cabaret Dinner Theatre
City Market
Cleartalk
Cottonwood Liquors
Deborah Braffett,
  Monument Realty
Garfield's Restaurant
Gene Taylor's Sportsman's
  Supply
Gladstone's Restaurant & Bar
Grande River Vineyards

Grand Valley Magazine
Grand Vista Hotel
Hill & Holmes Real Estate
IntelliTec
Main Street Bagels
Maptech
Monument Realty
Pantuso's Ristorante & Lounge
Peczuh Printing
St. Mary's Hospital
Studio 12 Styling Salon
Rocky Mountain Subaru
Winery Restaurant

Acknowledgements:
We could not have produced this book without the help of
many people who have given freely of their time, knowledge,
resources, skills and patience.

Special thanks to all the contributors, especially the U.S.
Forest Service, the Bureau of Land Management, the National
Park Service, and Maptech for providing the maps and
detailed backcountry information. All of these have been
invaluable resources.

Thanks to all the volunteers who have helped make, maintain,
and keep the trails beautiful for generations. They are usually well marked,
maintained, and easy to use. Please help keep these trails pristine, so that all
those who come after you can have that same feeling of being the only one on
a trail in months.

Most importantly, we would like to thank our friends and family. They have
spent endless hours with us in the exploration of our surroundings. Without all
of them, the hundreds of miles over mountains, plateaus, and streams would
have been truly lonely indeed. And this guide could not have been completed
without their support, encouragement, information and assistance.

Disclaimer:
The outdoor activities discussed in this guide can be dangerous and might
result in bodily injury. It is strongly recommended the user know his or her
physical limitations and only undertake the trails that common sense dictates
are safe and reasonable. The authors disclaim all representations and warranties
to informational accuracy or injury resulting from the use of this guide. It is the
sole responsibility of the user to know the limits of his or her ability and not
base decisions on any ideas suggested in these pages, be it safety precautions,
trail descriptions or warnings. The user of this outdoor guide assumes all risks
associated with these activities.

Legend
There are several abbreviations or symbols we have used throughout this book
to make the large amount of information on the trails easier to understand.
These terms and symbols are explained below.

DT	Double track trail or road
ST	Single track trail
WA	Wilderness Area
WSA	Wilderness Study Area
CCNCA	Colorado Canyons National Conservation Area
LBCWSA	Wild Horse Range-Little Book Cliffs Wilderness Study Area

 Hiking/Running allowed

 Fishing allowed in the area

 Mountain Biking allowed

 X-country/Snowshoeing trail

 Camping allowed in the area

 Horseback riding allowed

Reading the Elevation

To give you a more complete idea of what a trail is really like, we have provided mileage estimates, trail descriptions and elevation gains. Just under the trail name, we have listed the elevation gain of the trail. This number represents the amount of climbing that occur on the trail. The first number represents the climb on the way out and the second number represents the climb on the way back. If there is no second number the trail is either a loop or there is little or no gain in elevation. The Leg Burner boxes provide additional elevation gain information, with a visual representation of the previous written elevation gain. When using these boxes as a guide, please pay careful attention to the elevation numbers listed on the left-hand side of the box. For example, a trail might gain 500 feet of elevation in the same distance that another trail gains 5,000 feet. Please consider all the provided information completely before taking on a trail.

Trail Etiquette

A trail is a pathway into a world unblemished by man's mechanical progress. It allows us a pleasurable way to immerse ourselves in the natural environment.

All outdoor sports leave a trace; the most evident influence is wider trails that damage surrounding ground cover. Other heinous deeds are the cutting of trees and bushes and dropping trash. It is not simply our enjoyment of excellent trails that should motivate our thinking, but protecting the trails. Go for a walk, run or horseback ride and look at the cirques, lakes and trees and appreciate these spectacular sights, sounds and smells without venturing off a designated trail. We can do all we need to from the confines of the trail, and simultaneously learn what flowers and trees are trailside, what creek flows from the distant mountain range and what animals live in the surrounding area.

Trail Etiquette:

- Stay on designated trails and do not shortcut switchbacks
- Walk on durable surfaces (drainages, rocks, snow) when a trail crosses a fragile area
- Never walk through foliage or fragile soil next to trails
- Never cut trees or pick wildflowers
- Do not use a motorized vehicle on a trail closed to them
- Never leave trash behind and pick up any trash you find
- Leave all trails in good shape, free of any signs of human interference
- Be friendly to other trail users
- Pack it in and pack it out - everything!

When we consider the whole scope of what we can do to help the natural world, trail etiquette is a small fraction. We can do so much more from recycling to volunteer trail building work, or donating funds to outdoor related associations. When we are friendly and thoughtful while enjoying trails, the experience has a twofold result: We protect our natural heritage and relish in sharing a healthy pastime.

contents

West

contents

North

contents

East

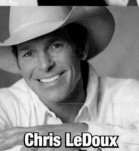

West

The Colorado National Monument is an area full of monolithic sandstone towers, arches, historical artifacts and petroglyphs. The trail systems move west past the Colorado National Monument to the classic Kokopelli Trail to Rabbit Valley then onward to Moab. The Monument shocks the senses with stoic pillars, sheer cliffs, balanced rocks and heavily used dirt playgrounds. Stunning alcoves and the sublime Colorado River are juxtaposed beside terra cotta and black striped sandstone cliffs. A masterful mix of sweeping singletrack trails is the last vestige of eroded hillsides before entering Utah. Experience ancient Indian petroglyphs and pictographs dating as far back as 1025 AD. This valley is rife with dinosaur fossils and the opportunity to see red-tail hawks, pronghorn antelope, mule deer and bald eagles. The lower elevation trails at 4,500 to 6,000 feet are available for winter or summer time enjoyment. The trails above the Monument offer cooler climates for the perfect summertime escape.

Studies show that mosquitoes prefer the color blue.
In the spring time, the high country can have an influx
of mosquitoes. Consider avoiding their favorite color
to help prevent those pesky bites.

mosquito

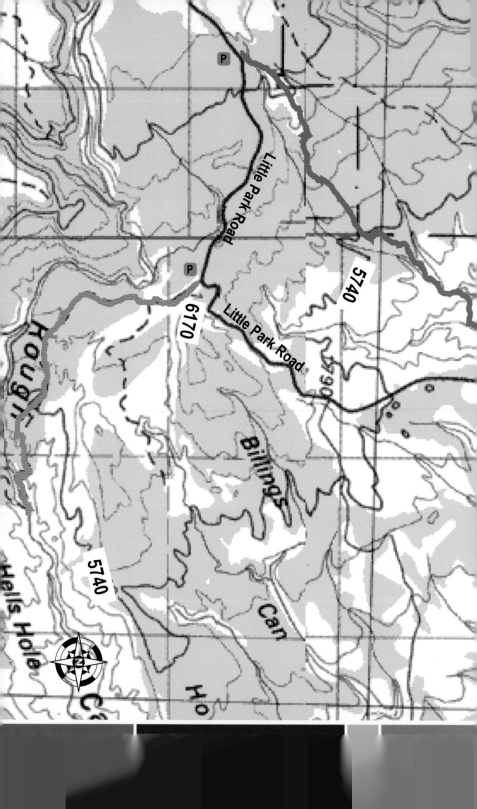

abeguache Trails

Monument Road

Canyon

Little Park Road

Monument Road

▲5410

Little Park Road

private property

p 30   The Ribbon

Andy's - Tabeguache Trails

Distance: 2.9 miles one way/ 5.8 miles out and back
Elevation Gain: 775 feet   **Use:** Moderate
Foot Difficulty: Moderate   **Biking Difficulty:** Moderate-Difficult

Trail Location: From downtown Grand Junction at the intersection of U.S. Hwy 6 & 50 and Broadway, follow Broadway west over the Colorado River and make a left (S) on Monument Road. Park on the left (S) at the Tabeguache Trailhead 2 miles along Monument Road. Andy's begins 1 mile along Eagle Tail.

West

Mileage Estimate

0.0-2.4m Turn to the right (W) and drop down a steep hill to the base of the canyon and through the creek bed. Drop down again to the base of another wash to The Ribbon junction.

2.4-2.9m Turn left (NE) at The Ribbon junction and climb up almost 500 feet and out to Little Park Road.

2.9-5.8m Turn around for the out and back or continue on The Ribbon or Eagle Wing.

Trail Description: Andy's takes you below Eagle's Wing and Eagle's Tail via a dry wash. A few steep drops will be encountered along Andy's. There are also very steep climbs out of The Ribbon onto Little Park Road. From Little Park Road many trail options are available. See the Tabeguache Trails map on page 17.

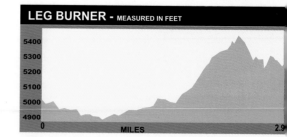

LEG BURNER - MEASURED IN FEET

5400	
5300	
5200	
5100	
5000	
4900	
0	MILES	2.9

HEALTHY

"A Healthy Alternative to Fast Foods"

644 North Avenue, Chinle Plaza, Grand Junction

257-9229

www.bocaza.com

Eagle Tail - Tabeguache Trails

Distance: 2.1 miles one way/ 4.2 miles out and back
Elevation Gain: 800 feet   **Use:** Moderate
Foot Difficulty: Moderate   **Biking Difficulty:** Moderate-Difficult

Trail Location: From downtown Grand Junction at the intersection of U.S. Hwy 6 & 50 and Broadway, follow Broadway west over the Colorado River and make a left (S) on Monument Road. Park at the Tabeguache Trailhead 2 miles along Monument Road on the left (S) side of the road.

West

Mileage Estimate

0.0-1.0m Go south out of the parking area and make a right (W) along the northernmost ridge. Climb the narrow ST to Andy's junction.

1.0-1.25m Continue straight up along the ridge.

1.25-2.1m Stay straight at this no name cutoff and continue uphill to the end of the trail and the Eagle Wing junction.

2.1-4.2m Head back or continue on Eagle Wing.

Trail Description: Eagle Tail is a rocky and narrow ST that offers amazing views of Colorado National Monument and the city of Grand Junction. It is a short trail with an elevation climb and technical sections. Andy's, Eagle Wing and the Eagle Wing Cutoff are all available from this trail.

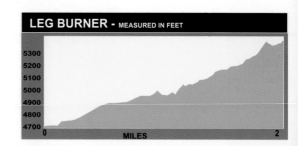

LEG BURNER - MEASURED IN FEET

5300
5200
5100
5000
4900
4800
4700
0   MILES   2

Eagle Wing/Eagle Wing Cutoff - Tabeguache Trails

Distance: 1 mile one way/ 2 miles out and back
Elevation Gain: 775 feet
Foot Difficulty: Moderate

Use: Moderate
Biking Difficulty: Moderate-Difficult

Trail Location: From downtown Grand Junction at the intersection of U.S. Hwy 6 & 50 and Broadway, follow Broadway west over the Colorado River and make a left (S) at Monument Road. Park on the left (S) at the Tabeguache Trailhead 2 miles along Monument Road. Eagle Wing begins about 500 yards along the Tabeguache and to the west. Eagle Wing Cutoff begins 1.6 miles west of the main parking area.

West

Mileage Estimate

0.0-0.4m From Eagle Wing Cutoff at the base of Widowmaker Hill, go to the right (W) along a tight ST. Move up and down through the trees to the Eagle Wing and Eagle Tail junction.

0.4-1.0m Take a left (SW) and climb a steep exposed section to the ridge and then to the crest of the trail.

1.0-2.0m Follow the trail down a loose and rocky section until reaching the Tabeguache just above Widowmaker Hill.

LEG BURNER - MEASURED IN FEET

Trail Description: Eagle Wing/ Eagle Wing Cutoff is a 2 mile trail along Tabeguache at the base of Widowmaker Hill. It rises steeply to the top of the ridge and has great views of the Monument, Grand Junction and The Ribbon. Many options exist on either exits of the trail. See Tabeguache Trails map on page 17.

Gunny Loop - Tabeguache Trails

Distance: 9 mile loop
Elevation Gain: 1,500 feet
Foot Difficulty: Moderate

Use: Moderate-Heavy
Biking Difficulty: Moderate-Difficult

Trail Location: From downtown Grand Junction at the intersection of U.S. Hwy 6 & 50 and Broadway, follow Broadway west over the Colorado River 0.8 miles and make a left (S) at Monument Road. Park on the left (S) at the Tabeguache Trailhead 2 miles into Monument Road.

Mileage Estimate

0.0-1.6m Head out of the main parking area along the well marked Tabeguache Trail to Widowmaker Hill.

1.6-2.4m Turn left (SE) and up until it levels off. Continue straight at the Eagle Wing junction and then out to Little Park Road.

2.4-3.1m Turn right (SW) onto the pavement and follow it to Little Park Road Staging Area/First Flats.

3.1-4.2m Follow this well marked dirt road to the turn-around for cars. At the back of the turn-around, follow the rocky 4x4 road downhill to the well-marked ST.

4.2-6.8m Turn left (N) at the ST to the prairie, through a canyon and over the ridge onto Little Park Road. Look for the trail on the left (N) side of the road.

6.8-7.4m Cross the road and connect with the Lower Gunny Loop ST, then up and down to the DT.

7.4-8.0m Turn left (SW), follow the DT a short distance, then right (W) on the ST up and over the hill. On the other side of the trail junction, go down the hill.

8.0-8.3m Stay straight at the junction and follow the trail back up to a ridge. Make a left (W) then a quick right (N) to the bentonite hill drop off.

8.3-9.0m Veer right (N) at the bottom, connecting with the Tabeguache Trail and follow it back to the parking area.

Trail Description: Gunny Loop can be mixed and matched with Andy's, Eagle Tail/Eagle Wing and Lunch Loop. It has panoramic views of the Grand Junction area and the Book Cliffs. Mountain bikers beware of the section at mileage 4.2 through 6.8 because it is the most technical along the trail. There are also a couple of almost straight up and down sections where mountain bikers may want to use extra caution and walk.

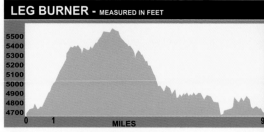

LEG BURNER - MEASURED IN FEET

5500	
5400	
5300	
5200	
5100	
5000	
4900	
4800	
4700	

0   1   MILES   9

Holy Cross - Tabeguache Trails

Holy Cross is currently closed for rebuilding. It is expected to open in the summer of 2002.

Trail Location: From downtown Grand Junction at the intersection of U.S. Hwy 6 & 50, take Broadway west to Monument Road and turn left (S). Follow Monument Road for 2.2 miles to the parking area on the left (S).

West

Trail Description: When Holy Cross reopens in this area, it will be for both mountain biking and hiking. It got its name because it passed by an actual wooden cross. There are no signs announcing that this trail is closed, so please don't use this trail until it reopens.

Lunch Loop - Tabeguache Trails

Distance: 3.2 mile loop
Elevation Gain: 670 feet   **Use:** Moderate-Heavy
Foot Difficulty: Easy-Moderate   **Biking Difficulty:** Moderate

Trail Location: From downtown Grand Junction at the intersection of U.S. Hwy 6 & 50 and Broadway, follow Broadway west over the Colorado River and make a left (S) on Monument Road. Park on the left (S) at the Tabeguache Trailhead 2 miles along Monument Road.

West

Mileage Estimate

0.0-1.6m   Follow the Tabeguache Trail up to Widowmaker Hill.

1.6-3.2m   Turn around at the base of Widowmaker Hill and head back to the parking area.

Trail Description: Lunch Loop is a moderate climb up the Tabeguache Trail, to the base of Widowmaker Hill, and then back down. It was named Lunch Loop because it takes an average person an hour to complete it, therefore allowing them to get a quick workout on their lunch break. There are many different local versions of this trail but the most consistent one is this out and back.

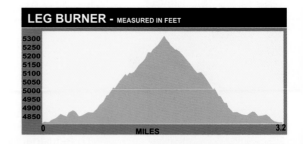

LEG BURNER - MEASURED IN FEET

5300
5250
5200
5150
5100
5050
5000
4950
4900
4850

0   MILES   3.2

Explore

Explore the Grand Junction area...

...with your friend in the business.

When it comes to finding just the right home or property, Deb will go the extra mile for you.

a friend in the business | **Deborah Braffett**

Mira Monte Canyon - Tabeguache Trails

Distance: 5.0 mile loop
Elevation Gain: 1,100 feet
Foot Difficulty: Easy-Moderate

Use: Heavy
Biking Difficulty: Moderate

Trail Location: From downtown Grand Junction at the intersection at U.S. Hwy 6 & 50 and Broadway, follow Broadway west over the Colorado River and make a left (S) on Monument Road. Follow Monument Road 0.7 miles and take a second left (S) onto South Redlands Road. Then veer right (S) at the Y intersection onto Mira Monte Road. Park in the small parking area at the end of Mira Monte Road where it turns into a dirt road. This is private property, so please be courteous.

Mileage Estimate

0.0-1.1m The trail begins south downhill around the base of a ridge and goes west through a canyon wash and a section of boulders to a trail junction.

1.1-1.4m Turn right (NW) up and over a ridge to the top and the bentonite hill.

1.4-2.3m Drop down this steep section and turn left (W) at the base and join the Tabeguache. Continue up the DT to the next trail junction just above the Lemon Squeezer section.

2.3-2.5m Turn right/SW and continue the DT to the base of Widowmaker.

2.5-3.8m Turn around and continue straight through Lemon Squeezer and along a ridge to the next trail junction.

3.8-4.9m Continue straight and begin a gentle uphill climb atop the ridge above and south of Mira Monte Canyon. As the trail tops off, descend quickly to the base of Mira Monte Canyon and back to the beginning of the loop.

4.9-5.0m Follow the trail back around the ridge and up to the parking area.

LEG BURNER - MEASURED IN FEET

5200
5100
5000
4900
4800
4700

0   MILES   5

Trail Description: Mira Monte makes a loop with the Tabeguache along a ridge, and through Mira Monte Canyon and through Lemon Squeezer. The Lemon Squeezer is a section of rock with large boulders you have to "squeeze" through.

The Ribbon - Tabeguache Trails

Distance: 4.0 miles one way/ 8.0 miles out and back
Elevation Gain: 1,700 feet   **Use:** Moderate
Foot Difficulty: Moderate-Difficult   **Biking Difficulty:** Difficult

Trail Location: Around 7 miles from Grand Junction, from the intersection of U.S. Hwy 6 & 50 and Broadway. Follow Broadway west and make a left (S) onto Monument Road. Then make another left (S) onto D Road. Follow D for 1.2 miles until it turns into Rosevale Road. Then turn right (SW) onto Little Park Road to the Little Park Road Staging Area/First Flats.

West

Trail Description: The Ribbon drops into a small canyon then makes its way up long, steep climbs over slickrock. It is flat across the top so it has some amazing views. It is strongly recommended for mountain bikers to take Little Park Road for the 3.2 miles to the parking area. If they try to backtrack the trail, they might miss some of the crucial turns and become lost.

Mileage Estimate

0.0-0.3m Leave the Little Park Road Staging Area and go downhill and to the right (NE).

0.3-0.8m Turn left (W) off the road onto an ST and begin this very steep and loose downhill to Andy's junction.

0.8-1.9m Turn left (E) up the dry wash, then up and over another hill with trees. Follow the ST to the section of slickrock.

1.9-2.4m At the slickrock, veer left (S) and up another larger section of slickrock. Follow the trail over a ridge and into a sandy section.

2.4-3.0m Turn right (SW) up the large slickrock section to where the trail veers left (SW).

3.0-3.4m After reaching some melted slickrock formations, head to the last humongous slab of slickrock.

3.4-4.0m The trail continues off this slickrock ridge and makes its way to the parking area.

4.0-8.0m Head back or continue down Little Park Road.

LEG BURNER - MEASURED IN FEET

MILES

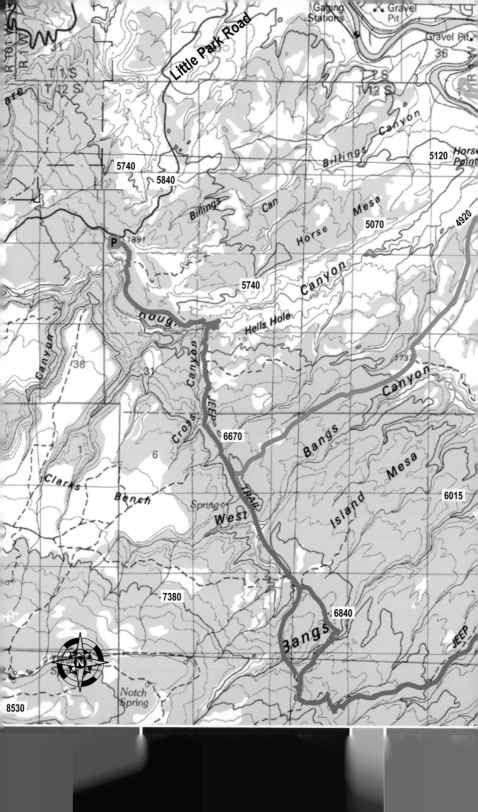

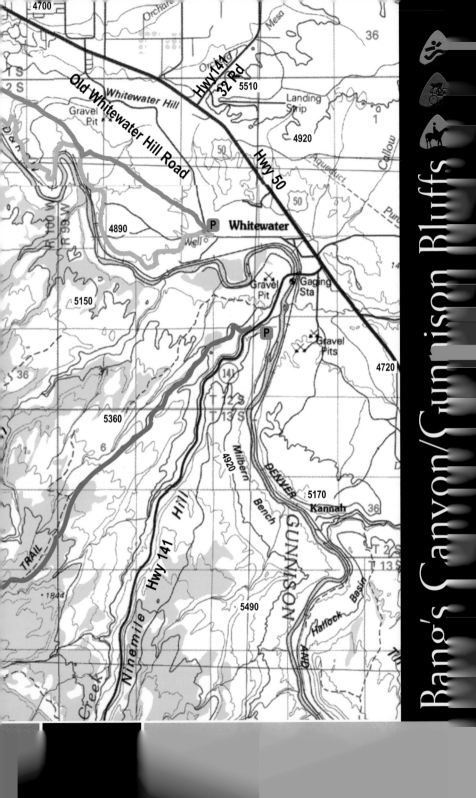

Gunnison Bluffs

Distance: 8 miles one way/ 16 miles out and back
Elevation Gain: 1,150 feet/ 1,100 feet   **Use:** Heavy
Foot Difficulty: Easy-Moderate   **Biking Difficulty:** Moderate

Trail Location: access 1 Travel south of downtown Grand Junction on Hwy 50 for 5.75 miles and make a right (SW) onto the Old Whitewater Road/Landfill Road. Follow the dirt road for 2.2 miles and past the dump site to the Gunnison Bluffs/Spanish Trail Parking Area.
access 2: Travel south of Grand Junction 3.3 miles and make a right (S) onto 28 1/2 Road. Then make an immediate left (SE) onto B Road. Make another immediate right (SW) just before meeting 28 1/2 Road again. Park at the Gunnison Bluffs/ Spanish Trailhead.

West

Mileage Estimate (starting from access 1)

0.0-2.4m Begin in a southwesterly direction up and down along and above the Gunnison River.

2.4-2.9m At this area next to the riverbank and the railroad tracks, continue north into the small canyon and merge with Spanish Trail.

2.9-3.1m Climb out of this rocky steep hill to where the trail splits.

3.1-4.7m Veer left (W) and climb up and back onto the edge of the bluff then into another canyon.

4.7-6.0m Climb up and out of the canyon and atop the next bluff, continuing along the top.

6.0-6.8m The trail turns to the east and down to the Spanish junction.

6.8-8.0m The trails are together again on the way down the steep drop next to the private property fence and then to the residential area. Follow the Spanish Trail signs to the open field and the end of both trails.

8.0-16.0m This is the second access parking area so turn around unless you shuttled a car.

Trail Description: Gunnison Bluffs was frequently used in the 1800's by explorers on their way to New Mexico and California. Now it is traveled by locals and tourists visiting the area in the spring and fall. Make sure to bring plenty of water on a summer trip. There are awesome views of the Gunnison River and the Adobe Desert area throughout this rocky up and down ride. The trail also travels above the railroad tracks where trains pass by each day.

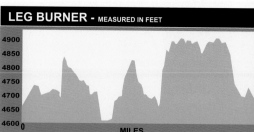
LEG BURNER - MEASURED IN FEET

Rough Canyon - Bang's Canyon

Distance: 2 miles one way/ 4 miles out and back
Elevation Gain: 120 feet/ 900 feet   **Use:** Moderate
Foot Difficulty: Easy-Moderate   **Biking Difficulty:** Moderate

Trail Location: Around 9 miles from Grand Junction at the intersection of U.S. Hwy 6 & 50, go west on Broadway. Turn left (S) onto Monument Road, then left (S) again onto D Road. Follow D Road for 1.2 miles until it turns into Rosevale Road. Then turn right (W) onto Little Park Road to the Bang's Canyon Parking Area at 5.3 miles.

West

Mileage Estimate

0.0-0.4m Head south out of the parking lot on a DT trail, and then uphill a short distance to the slickrock.

0.4-2.0m At the slickrock, turn left (SE) and follow the cairns through the pockets of sand and trees to the canyon bottom.

2.0-4.0m Turn around or try Rough Canyon to Whitewater.

Trail Description: Rough Canyon is a small portion of the Tabeguache Trail. In the spring and early summer, a waterfall adds a special treat at the bottom of Rough Canyon. For more miles, continue on Rough Canyon to Whitewater.

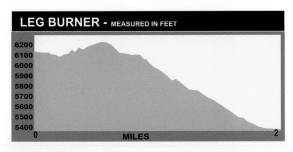

LEG BURNER - MEASURED IN FEET

Rough Canyon to Whitewater - Bang's Canyon

Distance: 18.5 miles one way/ 37 miles out and back
Elevation Gain: 2,500/4,000 feet   **Use:** Moderate
Foot Difficulty: Easy-Difficult   **Biking Difficulty:** Moderate-Difficult

Trail Location: access 1 Around 9 miles from Grand Junction at the intersection of U.S. Hwy 6 & 50, go west on Broadway. Turn left (S) onto Monument Road, then left (S) again onto D Road. Follow D Road for 1.2 miles until it turns into Rosevale Road. Then turn right (W) onto Little Park Road to the Bang's Canyon Parking Area at 5.3 miles.
access 2 South on U.S. Hwy 50 to Whitewater. Make a right (SW) on State Route 141. Follow the highway for 1.4 miles to the trailhead on the north side of the road at the ladder fence crossing. Park in any nearby pullout.

West

Mileage Estimate (starting from access 1)

0-0.4m Go south out of the parking lot on a DT trail up to the slickrock.

0.4-2.0m At the slickrock, turn left (E) and follow the cairns through the pockets of sand and the trees to the bottom of the canyon.

2.0-4.5m Cross the dry creek bed and up to West Bang's Canyon junction.

4.5-4.9m Continue past West Bang's and the trail junction and the spring on the right (SW).

4.9-9.0m Continue straight and take the second right (SE) and climb to the top elevation of 7,250 feet where the trail turns east.

9.0-18.0m Turn left (E) near the top and then down the rocky and sometimes steep DT.

18.0-18.5m As the trail flattens, look for the trail heading off to the right (S). If you stay straight, the trail may run into private property. Follow along the switchbacks to Highway 141.

18.5-37.0m Turn around to complete the out and back.

Trail Description: Rough Canyon to Whitewater via Tabeguache is an old DT trail that overlaps the Rough Canyon into the mouth of Unaweep Canyon and Highway 141, through the pinyon trees and to the top elevation of over 7,200 feet. It can be a shuttle ride or a very long out and back with awesome views of Bang's Canyon and the Grand Valley. It is a loose, rocky trail with some trail markers. A side trip can be made to view the spring located at the 4.5 to 4.9 mile mark.

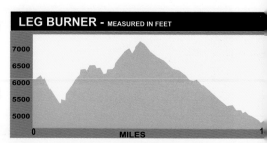

LEG BURNER - MEASURED IN FEET

7000
6500
6000
5500
5000

0   MILES   1

Right This Way, Your Table's Waiting...

DLER ON THE ROOF

OUTSTANDING PRODUCTIONS

In a relatively short time, the Cabaret has developed a strong reputation for high caliber professional productions of award-winning comedies and Broadway musicals 50 weeks out of the year, to over 40,000 audience members annually. The Cabaret was recently voted "Best In The West" for the third year in a row.

REVER PLAID

FINE DINING & SUPERIOR SERVICE

From the delicious, unique choice of entrees by Chef Danny Hayes to the excellent, friendly and courteous service, you'll feel like royalty at the Cabaret.

FOR ALL OCCASIONS

Always popular for company holiday parties, corporate meetings and special presentations, the Cabaret offers group ticket discounts, a full service bar, and homemade desserts, along with some of the best entertainment in the area, for up to 200 people.

And now for smaller group events, or just for a change of pace, the Spotlight Lounge offers the perfect compliment to the Cabaret. Featuring a rich, sophisticated atmosphere, fine dining, a luxurious parquet dance floor, and live piano and singing, the Spotlight is available for groups or private events for up to 150 people.

HOOL HOUSE ROCK LIVE!

NSENSE II

THE CABARET
DINNER THEATRE

Spend an Evening at
Grand Junction's Professional
Dinner Theatre

1-970-255-0999
1-877-255-0999

REFOOT IN THE PARK

Spanish Trail - Gunnison Bluffs

Distance: 4.9 miles one way/ 9.8 miles out and back
Elevation Gain: 600 feet/ 550 feet   **Use:** Heavy
Foot Difficulty: Easy   **Biking Difficulty:** Easy-Moderate

Trail Location: access 1 Travel south of downtown Grand Junction on Hwy 50 for 5.75 miles and make a right (SW) onto the Old Whitewater Road/Landfill Road. Follow the dirt road for 2.2 miles and past the dump site to the Gunnison Bluffs/Spanish Trail Parking Area.
access 2: Travel south of Grand Junction 3.3 miles and make a right (S) onto 28 1/2 Road. Then make an immediate left (SE) onto B Road. Make another immediate right (SW) just before meeting 28 1/2 Road again. Park at the Gunnison Bluffs/Spanish Trailhead.

West

Mileage Estimate (starting from access 1)

0.0-0.8m Start to the northwest along the wide trail and up toward the adobe plateaus in the distance.

0.8-1.9m The trail levels off here. Follow the signs to the trail junction.

1.9-2.0m Here the trail turns left (W) downhill into a small canyon and joins up with Gunnison Bluffs.

2.0-2.2m Climb this short, steep, and rocky hill to the next junction.

2.2-3.7m Veer right (N) here where the trails break away from each other and Spanish Trail continues north and becomes a bit rockier.

3.7-4.9m The trails come together again and go down a steep drop next to the private property fence and the residential area. Follow the Spanish Trail signs to the open field and the end of the trail.

4.9-9.8m Here is the second access parking area so turn around unless you shuttled a car.

Trail Description: Spanish Trail is a great outing in the spring and fall months, a bit toasty in the summer. It is a wide trail with more than enough room to move, but can be a bit rocky at times around the up and down hill areas. The northern branch of the Spanish Trail was used as hunting grounds by Ute tribes and also by early explorers on the way to New Mexico and California.

LEG BURNER - MEASURED IN FEET

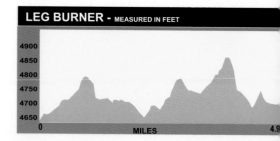

West Bang's Canyon - Bang's Canyon

Distance: 6 miles one way/ 12 miles out and back
Elevation Gain: 300 feet/ 1,675 feet   **Use:** Light
Foot Difficulty: Moderate
Biking Difficulty: Moderate-Difficult

Trail Location: Around 9 miles from Grand Junction at the intersection of U.S. Hwy 6 & 50, go west on Broadway. Turn left (S) onto Monument Road, then left (S) again onto D Road. Follow D Road for 1.2 miles until it turns into Rosevale Road. Then turn right (W) onto Little Park Road to the Bang's Canyon Parking Area at 5.3 miles. West Bang's begins 4.5 miles along Rough Canyon to Whitewater via the Tabeguache on the left (S) side.

Mileage Estimate

0.0-0.15m Begin by climbing uphill to the trail's highest point.

0.15-3.1m Go down the sometimes rocky trail along the left (N) side of West Bang's Canyon to a trail junction.

3.1-6.0m Turn left (NE) at this junction with the trail and drop down to where the trail ends just before the Gunnison River.

6.0-12.0m Turn around and climb back up.

Trail Description: West Bang's follows the canyon eastward until meeting up with the Gunnison River. That beginning section of the trail is an uphill climb to 6,600 feet but is worth it with the breathtaking views of the Grand Mesa and the floor of the Grand Valley. If you have a 4x4 high clearance vehicle, you can drive the 4.5 miles from the West Bang's Parking Area to the start of West Bang's.

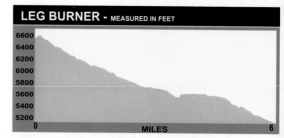

LEG BURNER - MEASURED IN FEET

6600
6400
6200
6000
5800
5600
5400
5200
0   MILES   6

Dinosaur Hill - Grand Junction River Front Trails - CCNCA

Distance: 1 mile loop
Elevation Gain: Light
Foot Difficulty: Easy

Use: Moderate-Heavy

Trail Location: From downtown Grand Junction, travel west on Broadway/Hwy 340 for 11.3 miles and turn right (NE) at the Dinosaur Hill sign. Follow the dirt road to the parking lot. From Fruita, travel south on I-70 for 1.5 miles and then turn left (NE) at the sign to the parking area.

Trail Description: Dinosaur Hill has 10 points of interest where paleontologists found and researched the existence of dinosaur fossils back in the early 1900's. It is a maintained trail that travels up a gentle incline, making it an ideal trail for kids, pets and all those with a dinosaur fascination.

West

Redland's Loop -Grand Junction River Front Trails

Distance: 8 plus miles
Elevation Gain: Light
Foot Difficulty: Easy

Use: Heavy
Biking Difficulty: Easy

Trail Location: access 1 Take Broadway from downtown just under a mile to Power Road and turn right (N). Follow Power Road for a short distance then veer left (W) onto Dike Rd and park in the few designated areas.
access 2 Travel along Broadway from downtown Grand Junction and turn right (N) onto River Road. Follow River Road for 2.8 miles and park at one of the locations along the road.

Trail Description: Access 1 takes you to a section of the Redlands Loop that is also known as the Audubon Trail. **Access 2** takes you to a different section of the Redlands loop also known as the Blue Heron Trail. This loop follows along the river, and offers views of wildlife and several kinds of birds. There are also picnic areas and some great fishing spots at the Connected Lakes. The path is paved so you can rollerblade on it as well.

Blue Heron

Rigg's Hill - Grand Junction River Front Trails

Distance: 0.75 mile loop
Elevation Gain: Moderate   **Use:** Moderate
Foot Difficulty: Easy-Moderate

Trail Location: 3.9 miles along Broadway from downtown Grand Junction and make a left (SW) on South Broadway. Follow South Broadway for 0.6 miles and park at the trailhead on the right (N) side of the road.

Trail Description: Riggs Hill is a great trail for a quick hike up and around the hill to view the 8 points of interest. This trail used for dinosaur research winds up, down and around the hill, and has a couple of areas of difficult hiking. Taking all of the trails in this area can make the miles add up to over 2 miles, but has some great views of the Redlands area and beyond.

West

Watson Island - Grand Junction River Front Trails

Distance: 3 plus miles
Elevation Gain: feet   **Use:** Heavy
Foot Difficulty: Easy

Trail Location: South of downtown Grand Junction on Highway 6 & 50 just on the either side of the 5th Street Bridge that travels over the railroad. Then make a left (E) on Struthers and park.

Trail Description: Watson Island is another river front park area just before the Gunnison River connects to the Colorado River. It travels along both sides of the Colorado River, and also the Old Mill Bridge on the north side of the Colorado.

Colorado National Monument

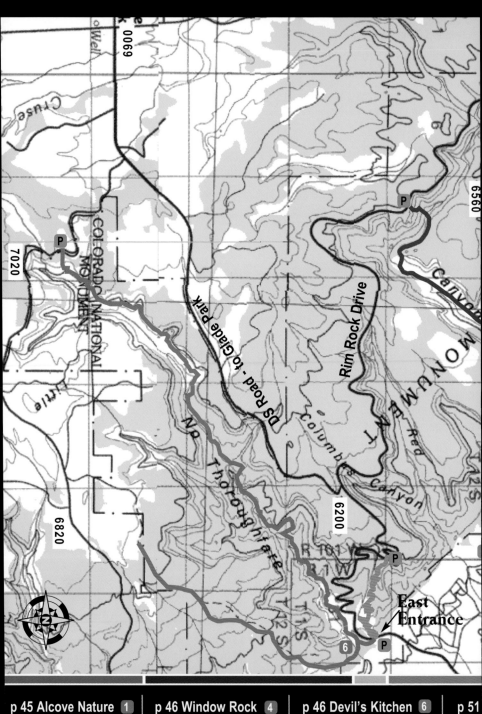

W. Glade Park Rd.

Rim Rock Drive

5740

MONUMENT MESA

COLORADO NATIONAL

Monument Canyon

Gold Star Can.

North

Enula

PACK TRAIL

Kodels

Visitor Center

West Entrance

4720 HWY 340

Broadway

Entrance

E. Pt.

PACK TRAIL

Canal

Aqueduct

S. Broadway

4690

P

Exit 15

STATE WILDLIFE WALKER AREA

Wildwood Dr.

S. Broadway

4800

Limekiln

Canal

Broadway

Redlan

Riggs Hill

South Camp Rd

R 101 W

R 1 W

Gravel Pit

400

R 2 W

R 1 W

70

31

Appleton

36

Reading Strip

T 11 S

T 1 N

Colorado National Monument

Below is a list of short, ideal family hikes in the Colorado National Monument that are 2 miles or less. We have created a map on the preceding page to help with the location of these trails and others on the Monument. For more details on these trails, ask for a map at the Visitor Center or at either entrance. Please note that these trails are for foot traffic only. Also, there are no dogs allowed on any of the trails in the Colorado National Monument, and camping is only allowed in organized campgrounds.

Alcove Nature

Trail Location: Across the road from the Visitor Center, 4.4 miles from the Colorado National Monument's west entrance on Rim Rock Drive.

Trail Description: Alcove Nature is a 2 mile out and back trail just below the Black Ridge Trail and along Kayenta Bench.

Canyon Rim

Trail Location: At the Visitor Center, 4.4 miles from the Colorado National Monument's west entrance and 18.5 miles from the east entrance on Rim Rock Drive.

Trail Description: Canyon Rim is a simple 1 mile out and back along the cliff edge. It has outstanding views at the Book Cliff Viewing Area and of Wedding Canyon.

C.C.C

Trail Location: 14.6 miles from the Colorado National Monument's east entrance or 8.3 miles from the west entrance on Rim Rock Drive. C.C.C Trail is just across the road from Monument Canyon.

Trail Description: C.C.C. links the Black Ridge to Monument Canyon. There are distant views of the San Juan Mountains at the Black Ridge junction. A good trail for those who don't want to commit to the longer Black Ridge or Monument Canyon.

Coke Ovens

Trail Location: 14.6 miles from the east entrance of the Colorado National Monument or 8.3 mile from the west entrance on Rim Rock Drive. It begins a short way along Monument Canyon.

Trail Description: It is a short 1 mile out and back that gently descends to an overlook with spectacular views of the rounded Coke Ovens rock formation and the Monument.

Devil's Kitchen

Trail Location: 0.2 miles from the east entrance to the Colorado National Monument. Park on the left (E) side of Rim Rock Drive. The is on the left (S) a half mile up No Thoroughfare Canyon.

Trail Description: A 1.5 mile out and back that combines well with No Thoroughfare Canyon. It is easy to lose your footing along this loose rocky trail, especially close the top, so be careful.

Window Rock

Trail Location: Just east of the Visitor Center, 4.4 miles from the Colorado National Monument's west entrance and 18.5 miles from the east entrance on Rim Rock Drive.

Trail Description: Window Rock is a short and level half mile loop through pinyons and juniper trees to an overlook with excellent views of Independence Monument, Wedding and Monument Canyons.

Ottos Trail

Trail Location: 5.4 miles from the Colorado National Monument's west entrance and 17.5 miles from the east entrance on Rim Rock Drive.

Trail Description: Ottos Trail is a 1 mile out and back downhill trail to the Pipe Organs and several other rock formations like the Monument Rock and the Coke Ovens.

Distance: 5.5 miles one way/ 11 miles out and back
Elevation Gain: 1,450 feet / 700 feet   **Use:** Moderate
Foot Difficulty: Moderate

Trail Location: access 1 Colorado National Monument's west entrance is 12 miles from Grand Junction and 2 miles from Fruita via Highway 340/Broadway. Continue through the entrance on Rim Rock Road for 4 miles to the Visitor Center on the left (S). Black Ridge starts across the road from the Visitor Center.
access 2 Across the road from the Liberty Cap parking lot off Rim Rock Drive, 12.2 miles from the east entrance and 10.7 miles from the west entrance.

West

Mileage Estimate (starting from access 1)
0.0-0.5m Follow the trail uphill from the other side of the road at the Visitor Center.

0.5-3.25m Follow the switchbacks uphill and onto BLM land for 2 miles. Then the trail goes the Colorado National Monument, over a fence and to the trail junction. C.C.C. is to the left (SE).

3.25-4.0m Stay straight uphill to the highest point below the Black Ridge.

4.0-5.5m Hike along the downhill section to the end of the trail on Rim Rock Drive.

5.5-11.0m Turn around here and head back, or try Liberty Cap.

Trail Description: Black Ridge runs atop the Monument through a portion of BLM land and then below the Black Ridge. It is a combination ST and DT with gentle ups and downs and sensational views of Utah, the Grand Valley and the San Juan Mountains.

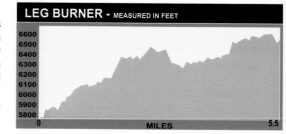

LEG BURNER - MEASURED IN FEET

Liberty Cap - Colorado National Monument

Distance: 7 miles one way/ 14 miles out and back
Elevation Gain: 2,200 total   **Use:** Moderate
Foot Difficulty: Moderate-Difficult

Trail Location: access 1 Take Broadway west to the Redlands for about 3.5 miles to a left (W) on South Broadway. Follow South Broadway 1.5 miles and just past Rigg's Hill, then turn left (S) on Wildwood Drive. Once on Wildwood Drive, make a quick right (SW) to the Liberty Cap/Ute Canyon Trailhead parking area on the right (W) side of the road.
access 2 Located on Rim Rock Road in the Colorado National Monument, 10.7 miles from the west entrance and 12.2 miles from the east entrance.

Mileage Estimate (starting from access 1)

0.0-0.7m The trail starts out of the parking area up the desert prairie and through a rocky section.

0.7-1.0m Just after the trail works its way against the rock wall, climb up a very steep and loose section for the next half-mile until reaching a trail junction. Take a right (NW) on Liberty Cap. Ute Canyon goes off to the left (SE).

1.0-1.5m The trail continues its difficult ascent up the Monument wall with good exposure and great views. Be careful.

1.5-7.0m Trek across the sandstone area following the cairns until joining the DT trail that gradually winds its way through the juniper trees. Reach the top at the trailhead parking area. Here you can continue on the Black Ridge Trail by crossing Rim Rock Road. Black Ridge will take you to the visitor's center. See map: pg 43 & Black Ridge description on pg 47.

7.0-14.0m Head back to the parking area unless you shuttled a car.

Trail Description: Liberty Cap is a difficult, tricky and technical trail up and down the face of the Monument wall for 1.5 miles. Be careful because parts of this trail requires agility for the some climbing. Once past the wall, take in the fabulous views of the sandstone formations, especially the cap rock pictured above from which the trail got its name. For the next 5.5 miles, the trail gradually works it way up through the juniper trees and yucca bushes to the western trailhead along the Rim Rock Drive. If you park at the Monument trailhead, this 5.5 mile stretch is a great cross country skiing trail.

LEG BURNER - MEASURED IN FEET

"WE KNOW Monument Country BEST!"

"Experienced Professional Service Since 1973"

monument
Realty, Inc.

- Residential
- Farm/Ranch
- Recreational
- Commercial
- New Home Construction
- Property Management
- Investments

970 **243-4890**
800-748-1225
Fax 241-6743

759 Horizon Drive, Suite A
Grand Junction, CO 81506
(Airport Exit just South of the Grand Vista Hotel)

web:www.monumentrealty.com
email:info@monumentrealty.com

Monument Canyon - Colorado National Monument

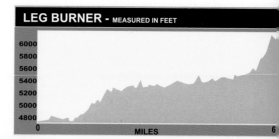

Distance: 6 miles one way/ 12 miles out and back
Elevation Gain: 2,250 feet   **Use:** Moderate-Heavy
Foot Difficulty: Moderate-Difficult

Trail Location: access 1 From the intersection of Broadway and U.S. Hwy 6 & 50 in Grand Junction, take Broadway west for 7.8 miles and turn left (NW) onto Fawn Lane. The parking lot is at the end of the road.
access 2 The upper trailhead is located 14.6 miles from the Colorado National Monument's east entrance or 8.3 miles from the west entrance on Rim Rock Drive.

West

Mileage Estimate (starting from access 1)

0.0-0.8m The trail starts out of the parking lot with some easy ups and downs along a private property fence line.

0.8-2.0m As the trail veers right (W) the elevation and difficulty will increase because the trail becomes rocky. It eases up a bit as Independence Monument comes into view.

2.0-2.5m Make a left (W) toward the Monument as you come alongside the base.

2.5-3.5m Follow the trail down and around the south side of the Monument. The trail gains elevation slowly on the way toward the Kissing Couple formation.

3.5-5.0m The trail moves around a few more monuments as it climbs up toward Rim Rock Drive.

5.0-6.0m Here it rises 600 feet to the upper trailhead.

6.0-12.0m Return downhill to the parking area unless you shuttled a car.

Trail Description: Monument Canyon is often times rough and rocky, but has glorious views of Independence Monument and other towers. On the way to the top, the trail becomes hard to negotiate. At the top, there is a viewing area for the Coke Ovens. For a really long trek, cross Rim Rock Drive over to the C.C.C. and connect to Black Ridge.

LEG BURNER - MEASURED IN FEET

6000
5800
5600
5400
5200
5000
4800

0   MILES   6

No Thoroughfare Canyon - Colorado National Monument

Distance: 8.5 miles one way/ 17 miles out and back
Elevation Gain: 2,950 feet   **Use:** Light
Foot Difficulty: Difficult

Trail Location: access 1 Colorado National Monument's east entrance is 4 miles from Grand Junction. From downtown Grand Junction, at intersection U.S. Hwy 6 & 50, go west on Broadway. Follow Broadway and turn left (S) onto Monument Road. Follow Monument Road for 4 miles to the east entrance. No Thoroughfare Canyon is located 0.2 miles from the east entrance of the Colorado National Monument. Park on the left(E).
access 2 Take Rim Rock Drive from the east entrance 3.5 miles to East Glade Park Junction and turn left (S). Follow this road 4.3 miles and turn left (S) to Little Park Road/DS Road. Drive 1.4 miles and park along the boundary fence.

West

Trail Description: It is not advisable to go beyond the sections that are well maintained. Once these end, the trail is marked with sporadically placed cairns and has two waterfalls that are hard to get over. No Thoroughfare is for the gutsy adventurer who can climb, read maps, and is completely prepared for the tough 18 miles out and back. If you try this return trip, then be prepared for at least an 8 hour day.

Mileage Estimate

0.0-0.2m Go downhill to the right (SW) into the canyon wash.

0.2-2.0m Continue in the wash, past Devil's Kitchen trail junction to your left (S). Keep going until you reach the first waterfall. Look to the right (N) for the cairns marking the trail. Here the trail climbs around 400 feet straight up.

2.0-3.5m As you approach the top, the trail plateaus. Take a left (W) just before it heads back down into the canyon's streambed. If you get lost, go to the bottom and continue to the next waterfall.

3.5-7.5m Continue through the wash, and then again go to the right (NW) up and over the second waterfall. Now the trail works its way above the wash on the right (NW) hand side. Continue above the wash until you reach the steep V shaped gully.

7.5-8.5m Now go in and out of the deep gully as the trail travels through the center canyon to the maintained trail.

8.5-17.0m Have someone pick you up here, or turn around.

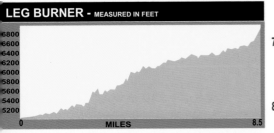

LEG BURNER - MEASURED IN FEET

52

Old Gordon - Colorado National Monument

Distance: 4 miles one way/ 8 miles out and back
Elevation Gain: 1,750 feet   **Use:** Moderate
Foot Difficulty: Moderate

Trail Location: Colorado National Monument's east entrance is 4 miles from Grand Junction. From downtown Grand Junction, at intersection U.S. Hwy 6 & 50, go west on Broadway. Follow Broadway to Monument Road. Turn left (S) and follow Monument Road for 4 miles to the east entrance. No Thoroughfare Canyon is located 0.2 miles from the east entrance of the Colorado National Monument. Park on the left side of the road. Old Gordon begins a short distance along No Thoroughfare Canyon.

West

Mileage Estimate

0.0-0.5m Start the trail downhill, past the No Thoroughfare Canyon split on the right/SW. Stay left (SE) until you get to the bottom of the canyon. The trail goes up to the right/S near the park boundary fence.

0.5-3.0m Continue up the slickrock above and to the left (S) of No Thoroughfare Canyon. The elevation gain to the top is consistent and moderate.

3.0-4.0m Here the trail bumps into an old fence post at the Colorado National Monument property line. Follow the small wash to the end of the trail and the permanent fence line.

4.0-8.0m Turn around here to complete the out and back.

Trail Description: Old Gordon is located the farthest southeast of all the trails in the Monument. It is a primitive and challenging trail to follow up and over the left or south side of No Thoroughfare Canyon. It has an elevation gain of 1,600 plus feet in 4 miles on the rocky, loose and solid slickrock.

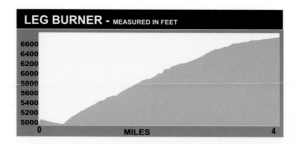

LEG BURNER - MEASURED IN FEET

6600
6400
6200
6000
5800
5600
5400
5200
5000
0   MILES   4

Serpent's Trail - Colorado National Monument

Distance: 2.25 miles one way/ 5.5 miles out and back
Elevation Gain: 1,200 feet   **Use:** Heavy
Foot Difficulty: Moderate

Trail Location: access 1 Colorado National Monument's east entrance is 4 miles from Grand Junction. From downtown Grand Junction, at intersection U.S. Hwy 6 & 50, go west on Broadway. Follow Broadway and turn left (S) onto Monument Road. Follow Monument Road for 4 miles to the east entrance. No Thoroughfare Canyon is located 0.2 miles from the east entrance of the Colorado National Monument. Park on the left (E) side of the road. Serpent's Trail is across the road at the bottom of the parking lot.
access 2 Continue past the access 1 parking, around 3 miles up Rim Rock Drive, through the tunnel, around the corner and to the left (S).

West

Mileage Estimate (starting from access 1)
0-2.25m   Cross the road at the end of the one way parking lot. Follow the wide, crooked trail among the rocks and slickrock to the top.

2.25-5.5m   Turn around here and head back down the Monument.

Trail Description: Serpent's Trail is a local favorite for walking. It follows an old access road to the top of the Monument. When it was first built, it was considered the most crooked trail in the world, with 50 switchbacks. The best time of day to travel this trail is at sunrise to soak in the sun kissed views and rocks.

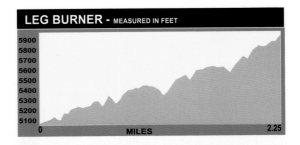

LEG BURNER - MEASURED IN FEET

5900
5800
5700
5600
5500
5400
5300
5200
5100

0   MILES   2.25

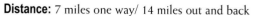

Ute Canyon - Colorado National Monument

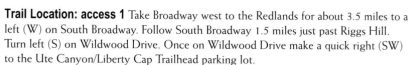

Distance: 7 miles one way/ 14 miles out and back
Elevation Gain: 1,950 feet   **Use:** Light
Foot Difficulty: Moderate-Difficult

Trail Location: access 1 Take Broadway west to the Redlands for about 3.5 miles to a left (W) on South Broadway. Follow South Broadway 1.5 miles just past Riggs Hill. Turn left (S) on Wildwood Drive. Once on Wildwood Drive make a quick right (SW) to the Ute Canyon/Liberty Cap Trailhead parking lot.
access 2 Located on the Rim Rock Road in the Colorado National Monument 13.8 miles from the west entrance and 9.1 miles from the east entrance.

West

Mileage Estimate (starting from access 1)

0.0-0.7m The trail starts out of the parking area up the desert prairie and through a rocky section.

0.7-1.0m Just after the trail works its way against the rock wall, climb up a very steep and loose section until reaching a trail junction.

1.0-2.0m Turn left (S) and work around the base of the rock wall into the canyon. The trail levels off and follows the dry wash.

2.0-5.5m Then weave in and out of the dry wash through the brush onto a narrow ST.

5.5-6.5m Veer right (NW) with the trail where the canyon heads to the northwest. Follow this uphill and back down into the dry wash.

6.5-7.0m Turn left (SW) up the canyon wall on the switchbacks to the top alongside Rim Rock Drive.

7.0-14.0m Follow the trail back down to the parking lot.

Trail Description: Ute Canyon is a narrow and undeveloped trail through cottonwood and willow trees. The trail and the surrounding area is usually soaked during the rainy season. Some arches are visible throughout the canyon. Near the top of the trail, on the switchbacks, there is a steep descent or ascent of around 600 feet up the canyon wall.

LEG BURNER - MEASURED IN FEET

(chart y-axis: 6400, 6200, 6000, 5800, 5600, 5400, 5200, 5000, 4800; x-axis: 0 to 7, MILES)

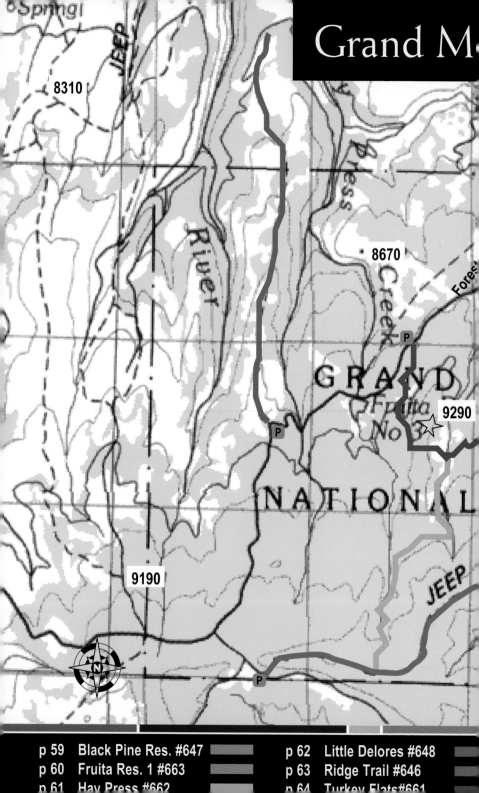

Grand M

8310

8670

Press

Creek

River

JEEP

Forest

P

GRAND

Fruita
No 3

9290

P

NATIONAL

9190

JEEP

P

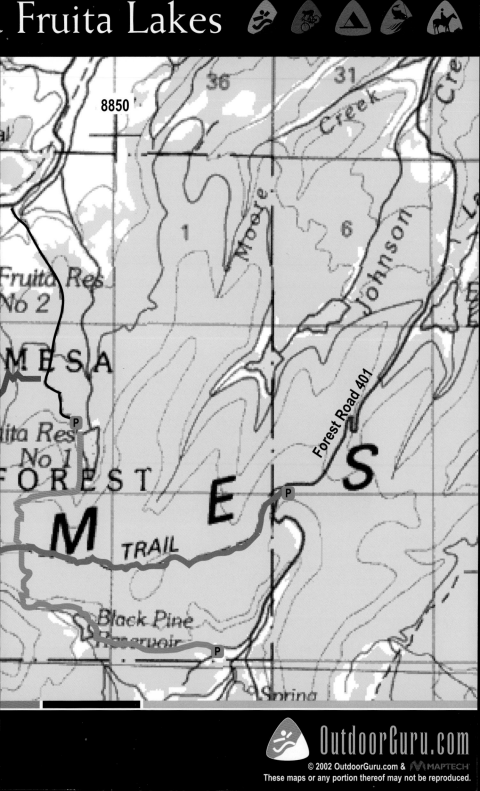

Black Pine Reservoir #647 - Grand Mesa/Fruita Lakes

Distance: 2 miles one way/ 4 miles out and back
Elevation Gain: 550 feet
Foot Difficulty: Easy-Moderate

Use: Light
Biking Difficulty: Moderate

Trail Location: From downtown Grand Junction, go west on Broadway to Monument Road. Follow Monument Road to the Colorado National Monument's east entrance. Follow the road up 4.3 miles to Glade Park Road and turn left (S). Follow Glade Park Road to the Glade Park General Store. Turn left (S) onto 16 Road for 8 miles, and veer left (SE) at the Y intersection. Follow the road for 2 miles, turning right (S) onto Eighteen Mile Road. Follow Eighteen Mile Road for 6 miles, then turn right (W) onto a dirt road. At the first right (W), turn and follow the road to a turn around. Park here. Black Pine Reservoir begins to the west.

West

Mileage Estimate

0.0-1.4m Begin along the boundary fence, then to the reservoir and around the reservoir's right (N) side.

1.4-2.0m Go uphill to the ridge top and the Ridge Trail and Fruita Reservoir #1 Trail junction.

2.0-4.0m Continue on either trail or head back.

Trail Description: Black Pine Reservoir makes its way up to Black Pine Reservoir on the mountain's southern face. Mosquitoes can be heavy in this area during the spring and summer. The trail is bordered by a private property fence to the South, so please stick to the trail area.

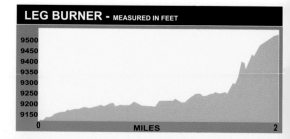

LEG BURNER - MEASURED IN FEET

Fruita Reservoir 1 #663 - Grand Mesa/Fruita Lakes

Distance: 1.5 miles one way/ 3 miles out and back
Elevation Gain: 400 feet   **Use:** Moderate
Foot Difficulty: Easy-Moderate   **Biking Difficulty:** Moderate

Trail Location: From downtown Grand Junction, go west on Broadway to Monument Road. Follow Monument Road to the Colorado National Monument's east entrance. Follow the road up 4.3 miles to the Glade Park Road and turn left (S). Follow Glade Park Road to the Glade Park General Store. Turn left (S) onto 16 Road for 8 miles, and veer right (W) at the Y intersection. Continue on this road for approximately 2.5 miles and turn left (S) at the Fruita Picnic Area. Follow this road 2 miles uphill to the trailhead.

Mileage Estimate

0.0-1.5m The trail follows along Fruita Reservoir #1, and then begins a moderate climb up and over to Ridge Trail/Black Pine Reservoir junction.

1.5-3.0m Head back or continue on the Ridge or Black Pine Reservoir trails.

Trail Description: Fruita Reservoir #1 is a short out and back trip through the aspens and up a few steep and rocky sections. There is an abundance of deer and elk along the way. It also makes a long loop with Ridge Trail, Hay Press, and Turkey Flats.

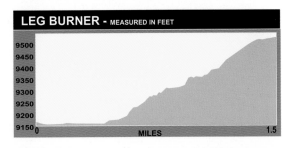

LEG BURNER - MEASURED IN FEET

(Elevation profile chart: y-axis 9150 to 9500 feet, x-axis 0 to 1.5 MILES)

Hay Press #662 - Grand Mesa/Fruita Lakes

Distance: 2 miles one way/ 4 miles out and back
Elevation Gain: 600 feet
Foot Difficulty: Easy-Moderate

Use: Moderate
Biking Difficulty: Moderate

Trail Location: access 1 From downtown Grand Junction, go west on Broadway to Monument Road. Follow Monument Road to the Colorado National Monument's east entrance. Follow the road up 4.3 miles to the Glade Park Road and turn left (S). Follow Glade Park Road to the Glade Park General Store. Turn left (S) onto 16 Road for 8 miles, and veer right (SW) at the Y intersection. Continue on for another 3.5 miles and turn left (SE) at this Y intersection. Park a half mile up the road. Hay Press starts 1.5 miles along Turkey Flats.
access 2 Located 1.1 miles along Ridge Trail. See Ridge Trail description on page 63.

Mileage Estimate

0.0-1.4m This trail begins 1.5 miles into Turkey Flats, making a left (NE) at the trail junction and climb uphill through the aspen and meadows.

1.4-2.0m Then it goes up some steep ledges and then to the Ridge Trail junction.

2.0-4.0m Head back or take the Ridge Trail.

Trail Description: Hay Press makes its way to the Ridge Trail in 2 miles. The ST is through the forest and is wet and muddy throughout mid summer. There are many fallen trees to climb over throughout this trail as well as mosquitoes to swat. At the end of this trail, continue with Ridge Trail, Fruita Reservoir #1, and Turkey Flats to complete a nice loop.

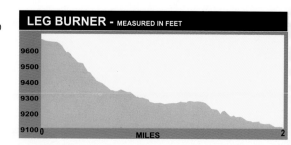

LEG BURNER - MEASURED IN FEET

Little Dolores #648 - Grand Mesa/Fruita Lakes

Distance: 2.6 miles one way/ 5.2 miles out and back

Elevation Gain: 100 feet/ 800 feet   **Use:** Moderate

Foot Difficulty: Easy-Moderate   **Biking Difficulty:** Moderate

Trail Location: From downtown Grand Junction, go west on Broadway to Monument Road. Follow Monument Road to the Colorado National Monument's east entrance. Follow the road up 4.3 miles to the Glade Park Road and turn left (S). Follow Glade Park Road to the Glade Park General Store. Turn left (S) onto 16 Road for 8 miles, and veer right (SW) at the Y intersection. Continue on this road for 4.7 miles to the trailhead on the right (W).

West

Mileage Estimate

0.0-2.6m   This DT trail makes its way down southern ridge of the Grand Mesa, then stops at the National Forest border. It can be very steep and rocky.

2.6-5.2m   There is no outlet here, so you must turn around when you reach the border of the National Forest.

Trail Description: Little Dolores is a short ATV trail downhill through the pines and aspens to overlook the Glade Park Area. The DT runs above and between the Little Dolores River and Hay Press Creek. It has wonderful views of the Little Dolores River and canyonlands to the northwest.

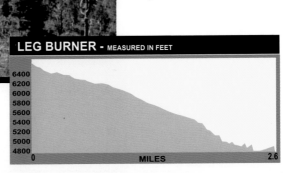

LEG BURNER - MEASURED IN FEET

| MILES |
| 6400 |
| 6200 |
| 6000 |
| 5800 |
| 5600 |
| 5400 |
| 5200 |
| 5000 |
| 4800 |
| 0   2.6 |

Ridge Trail #646 - Grand Mesa/Fruita Lakes

Distance: 4.4 miles one way/ 8.8 miles out and back
Elevation Gain: 320 feet /380 feet　**Use:** Moderate
Foot Difficulty: Easy-Moderate　**Biking Difficulty:** Easy-Moderate

Trail Location: access 1 From downtown Grand Junction, go west on Broadway to Monument Road. Follow Monument Road to the Colorado National Monument's east entrance. Follow the road for 4.3 miles to the Glade Park Road and turn left (S). Follow Glade Park Road to the Glade Park General Store. Turn left (S) onto 16 Road for 8 miles, and veer right (SW) at the Y intersection. Continue on for another 6.2 miles and turn left (SE) at this Y intersection. Park at the trail a half mile up the road.
access 2 At the 8 miles Y intersection, turn left (SE). Then at 2 miles, turn right (S) onto Eighteen Mile Road. Follow it for around 4.7 miles, turning right (W) to the Ridge Trailhead.

West

Mileage Estimate

0.0-0.6m Start out uphill along the rocky trail to the top elevation of 9,700 feet.

0.6-1.1m Follow the DT along the top to Hay Press on the left (N).

1.1-2.2m Stay straight and then downhill to Fruita Reservoir #1 and the Black Pine Reservoir junction.

2.2-4.4m Stay straight along the DT to the parking lot located at the eastern trailhead.

4.4-8.8m Turn around or continue onto Black Pine Reservoir via Eighteen Mile Road.

Trail Description: Ridge Trail is an ATV path along the top of the Grand Mesa, Fruita Lakes Division. It has colorful wildflowers and beautiful views of the Uncompahgre Plateau and the canyons near Gateway. This area of trails provides a great getaway from the summertime heat.

LEG BURNER - MEASURED IN FEET

9650
9600
9550
9500
9450
9400
0　　　　　　　MILES　　　　　4.4

Turkey Flats #661 - Grand Mesa/Fruita Lakes

Distance: 2.9 miles one way/ 5.8 miles out and back
Elevation Gain: 600 feet/300 feet   **Use:** Moderate
Foot Difficulty: Easy-Moderate   **Biking Difficulty:** Moderate

Trail Location: From downtown Grand Junction, go west on Broadway to Monument Road. Follow Monument Road to the Colorado National Monument's east entrance. Follow the road for 4.3 miles to the Glade Park Road and turn left (S). Follow Glade Park Road to the Glade Park General Store. Turn left (S) onto 16 Road for 8 miles, and veer right (SW) at the Y intersection. Continue on this road for 3.5 miles to the trailhead on the left. Park on the right (W).

West

Mileage Estimate

0.0-1.5m   Begin this moderate uphill climb past a small pond and some marshy areas. Then go up and over the mountain ridge to the Hay Press junction.

1.5-2.9m   The trail veers left (E) across a small creek. It levels off as it approaches a steep, loose and rocky downhill to the next creek crossing. Climb out and descend to the trail's end at FR 400.2d.

2.9-5.8m   Turn around or take a right (S) on the road to Fruita Reservoir #1.

Trail Description: Turkey Flats is a ST that makes its way through the aspens and open meadows of the Grand Mesa National Forest, Fruita Lakes Division. The blooming of the wildflowers and the brilliant colors on the trees as the season change can be enjoyed along this trail. During the rainy season, it becomes a very muddy trail. It makes a great trail by itself or can be a fun, large loop with Fruita Reservoir #1, Ridge Trail and Hay Press. See the map of Grand Mesa/Fruita Lakes Trails on page 57.

LEG BURNER - MEASURED IN FEET

9250	
9200	
9150	
9100	
9050	
9000	
8950	
8900	

0   MILES   2.9

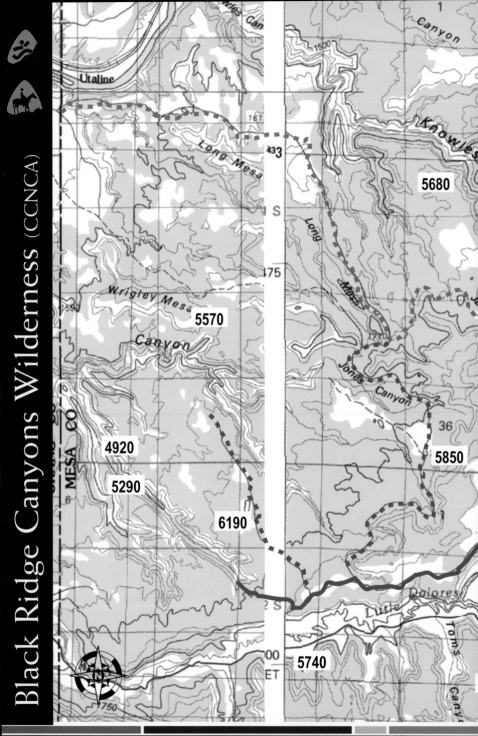

Black Ridge Canyons Wilderness (CCNCA)

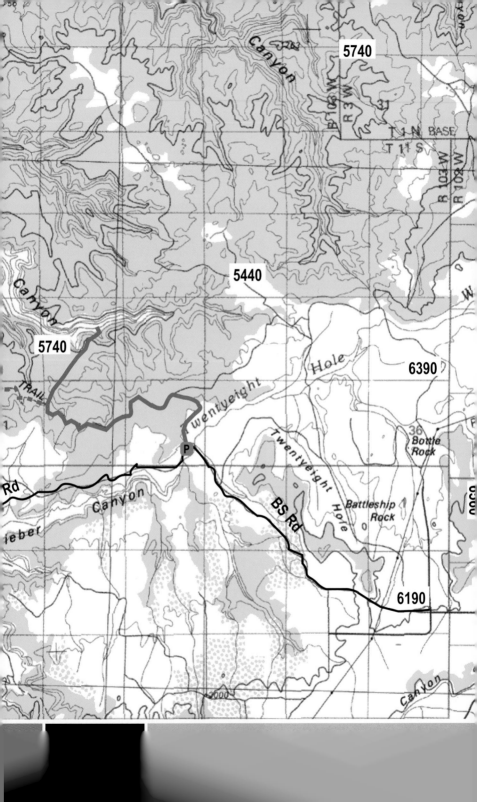

Jones Canyon - Black Ridge Canyons Wilderness (CCNCA)

Distance: 4.5 miles one way/ 9 miles out and back
Elevation Gain: 200 feet /600 total   **Use:** Moderate
Foot Difficulty: Easy-Moderate

Trail Location: Around 25 miles west of downtown Grand Junction on Broadway to Monument Road. Follow Monument Road to the Colorado National Monument's east entrance. Drive on Rim Rock Drive for 4.3 miles to the Glade Park Road turn off. Follow this turn off for 5.6 miles to the Glade Park General Store. Turn right (N) onto 16 Road and go a half mile and turn left (W) onto BS Road. Follow BS Road for 7.3 miles, staying straight and crossing over the cattle guard. Continue an additional 7.3 miles to the trailhead.

West

Mileage Estimate

0.0-2.5m   Right away, there is an elevation change along the sandy DT.

2.5-3.2m   Stay straight and follow the trail to the next junction. The trail to the right (W) is for the northern section of Jones Canyon and connects to Knowles Canyon Trail.

3.2-3.7m   Stay straight along the DT to the next trail junction. A right (NW) here will go to an interesting rock feature. This branch of the trail ends after 3 miles.

3.7-4.5m   Turn right (NW) off the DT and follow the trail downhill to the Jones Canyon Overlook and some great vistas.

4.5-9.0m   Head back here at the Jones Canyon Overlook where the trail ends.

Trail Description: Jones Canyon is a DT trail through the BLM Wilderness Study Area with plenty of exploring to be done on foot. A few other Jones Canyon trails branch out from the overlook trail. The trail runs along a plateau just above and north of Sieber Canyon and the Little Dolores River. Traffic is rare on this trail, because the road is choked with sticker weeds. A fire scorched its way through this section, so many charred trees line the trail.

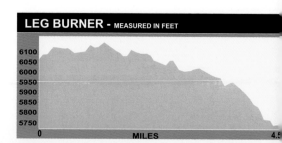

LEG BURNER - MEASURED IN FEET

6100
6050
6000
5950
5900
5850
5800
5750

0   MILES   4.5

Distance: 5.1 miles one way/ 10.2 miles out and back
Elevation Gain: 300 feet /1,675 total   **Use:** Light
Foot Difficulty: Moderate

Trail Location: Around 25 miles west of downtown Grand Junction on Broadway to Monument Road. Follow Monument Road to the Colorado National Monument's east entrance. Drive on Rim Rock Drive for 4.3 miles to the Glade Park Road turn off. Follow this turn off for 5.6 miles to the Glade Park General Store. Turn right (N) onto 16 Road and go a half mile and turn left (W) onto BS Road. Follow BS Road for 7.3 miles, staying straight and crossing over the cattle guard. Continue an additional 4.3 miles to the trailhead. Park on the right (N) side of the road.

West

Mileage Estimate

0.0-1.5m	Head out north through the open grasslands to a DT.
1.5-3.6m	Turn left (W) onto the DT and follow the winding switchback road down to the next junction.
3.6-4.7m	Make a right (NE) and continue to the rim of the canyon. Stay straight and continue along the southwest side of the canyon for another 12 miles to the Colorado River and the Utah border.
4.7-5.1m	Continue down a steep drop down into the bottom of the canyon.
5.1-10.2m	Head back or do some exploring along the floor of the canyon.

Trail Description: Knowles Canyon is near the western edge of the Black Canyons Wilderness/ CCNCA. It follows along and drops into the largest canyon in the north end of the Uncompahgre Plateau. This feature offers stunning canyon views. The longer 15 miles route to the Colorado River makes an ideal overnight hiking trip.

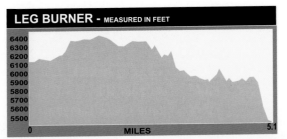

LEG BURNER - MEASURED IN FEET

6400
6300
6200
6100
6000
5900
5800
5700
5600
5500

0   MILES   5.1

68

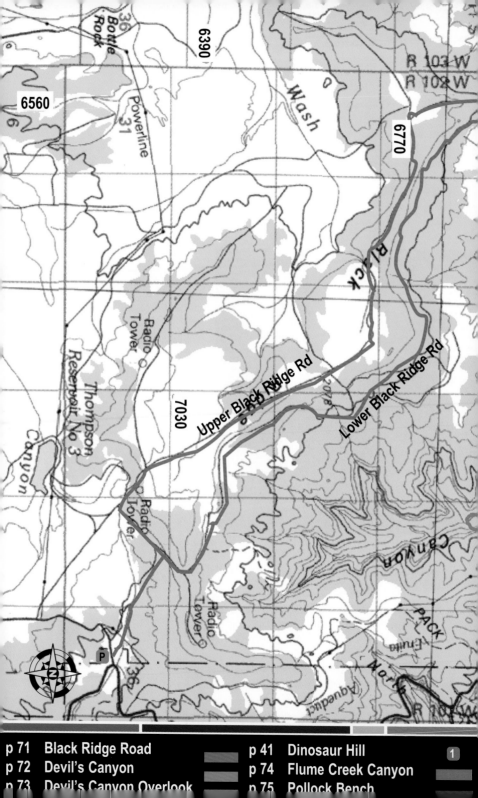

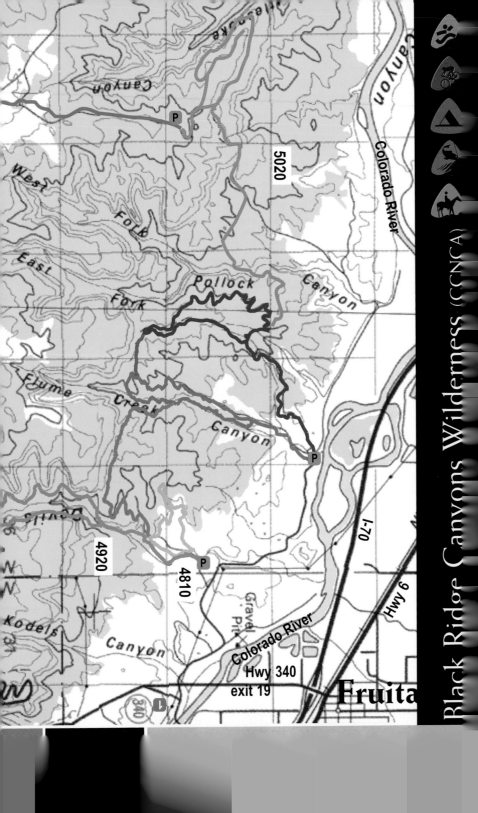

Canyon

P

5020

Colorado River

Canyon

West

Fork

Pollock

Canyon

East

Fork

Flume

Creek

Canyon

P

Devils

4920

P

4810

Kodels

Canyon

Gravel Pit

Colorado River

Hwy 340
exit 19

340

Fruita

I-70

Hwy 9

Black Ridge Canyons Wilderness (CCNCA)

Black Ridge Road - Black Ridge Canyons Wilderness (CCNCA)

Distance: 10.2 miles one way/ 20.4 miles out and back
Elevation Gain: 800 feet/1,050 feet   **Use:** Moderate
Foot Difficulty: Easy-Difficult   **Biking Difficulty:** Easy-Difficult

Trail Location: access 1 Colorado National Monument's west entrance on rim Rock Drive is 12 miles from Grand Junction and 2 miles from Fruita via Highway 340/Broadway. Continue on Rim Rock Drive for 11 miles to 16 Road. Turn right (W) onto 16 Road and go .25 miles to Black Ridge Road. Park here.
access 2 From downtown Grand Junction, at intersection U.S. Hwy 6 & 50, go west on Broadway. Follow Broadway to Monument Road. Turn left (S) and follow Monument Road for 4 miles to the east entrance. Continue along Rim Rock Drive for 12 miles to 16 Road. Turn left (W) onto 16 Road and go .25 miles to Black Ridge Road. Park here.

West

Mileage Estimate
(starting from access 1)

0.0-1.2m Uphill to approach to the ridge with the radio towers and trail junction.

1.2-2.0m Make a left (W) for the Upper Black Ridge Road. Off to the right (NE) is the Lower Black Ridge Road, which we have not described in this guide.

2.0-2.8m Turn right (NW) at the next junction and then climb up to the top elevation of over 7,000 feet.

2.8-7.6m The trail then plateaus across the Black Ridge to the next trail junction.

7.6-10.2m Take a right (N) and downhill over the roughest section of the road. At the end of the road is the Rattlesnake Arch.

10.2-20.4m Turn around or continue on Rattlesnake Arch.

Trail Description: The Upper Black Ridge Road is a tedious dirt road northwest atop the Black Ridge just above the Colorado National Monument. A great outing can be made by mountain biking the Black Ridge Road and then hiking Rattlesnake Arch. The Lower Black Ridge Road joins with the upper trail and can be used for the return trip.

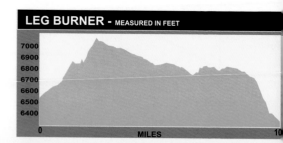

LEG BURNER - MEASURED IN FEET

7000
6900
6800
6700
6600
6500
6400

0   MILES   10

Devil's Canyon - Black Ridge Canyons Wilderness (CCNCA)

Distance: 7 mile loop
Elevation Gain: 1,200 feet   **Use:** Moderate
Foot Difficulty: Moderate

Trail Location: Travel southwest out of Fruita on Highway 340 for 1 mile to Kings View Road. Turn right (W) onto Kings View Road and go just over 1 mile to the Devil's Canyon sign. Turn left (W) at the sign and park a quarter mile up. The trailhead is at the end of the road near the gate.

West

Trail Description: Devil's Canyon loops up through a striking and beautiful sandstone canyon. It travels along a creek across the canyon and through the juniper trees. The unfinished and deserted cabin featured in the picture above can be seen at the halfway point of the trail. Don't be surprised if you encounter several horses or even a donkey. The D3 signs designate the trail for Devil's Canyon and the D1 represents the trail for Devil's Overlook.

Mileage Estimate

0.0-0.25m From the parking lot, follow the DT road to D4 and D1 junction. Veer left (S) on D1.

0.25-0.45m Continue on D1 a short distance to a left (S) on D3.

0.45-1.5m On D3, you cross a wooden bridge and turn right (SW) into the creek bed. Continue up along the creek bed to the next trail junction.

1.5-3.25m Make a left (S) at the D3 trail sign. The trail becomes increasingly difficult due to the increase in elevation. This trail makes its way up the left (E) side of the creek up and down through the canyon as you reach the cabin.

3.25-5.5m From the cabin, follow the trail as it winds up and down through the canyon back to the base of the creek bed.

5.5-7.0m Make your way back to the parking area along D3/D1.

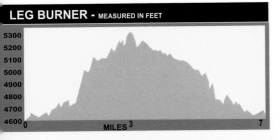

LEG BURNER - MEASURED IN FEET

5300	
5200	
5100	
5000	
4900	
4800	
4700	
4600	

0   MILES 3   7

Devil's Canyon Overlook - Black Ridge Canyons Wilderness (CCNCA)

Distance: 3.3 miles one way/ 6.6 miles out and back
Elevation Gain: 1,000 feet /850 feet   **Use:** Moderate
Foot Difficulty: Moderate

Trail Location: Travel southwest out of Fruita on Highway 340 for 1 mile to Kings View Road. Turn right (W) onto Kings View Road and go just over 1 mile to the Devil's Canyon sign. Turn left (W) at the sign and park a quarter mile up. The trailhead is at the end of the road near the gate.

West

Mileage Estimate

0.0-0.8m   From the parking lot, follow the D1 signs along the main DT road to the trail junction. The trail continues to the right (S) to the D4 and No Mountain Biking sign.

0.8-1.0m   Continue the DT road then veer left (W) at the D1 sign.

1.0-1.6m   Keep going along the DT into a small canyon where it makes a left (S) and switchbacks on the way up to the overlook.

1.6-2.4m   The trail turns right (W) through the junipers to the top elevation of 5,200 feet.

2.4-3.3m   The trail turns to the right (N) as it slides down to Flume Creek Canyon Trail junction. Add Flume Creek or the Pollock Bench for a day long excursion. See the Black Ridge Canyons Wilderness on page 69.

3.3-6.6m   Head back or continue on one of these other trails.

Trail Description: Devil's Canyon Overlook takes you up to a great overlook of the Grand Valley, Devil's Canyon and Flume Creek Canyon along a DT/ST through the junipers to Flume Creek Canyon. From Flume Creek, you can access Pollock Bench and its canyon. The D1 signs represent the trail for Devil's Canyon Overlook.

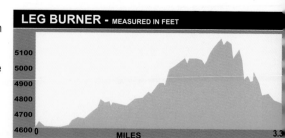

LEG BURNER - MEASURED IN FEET

Flume Creek Canyon - Black Ridge Canyons Wilderness (CCNCA)

Distance: 5 mile loop
Elevation Gain: 800 feet
Foot Difficulty: Easy-Moderate

Use: Moderate

Trail Location: Travel southwest out of Fruita on Highway 340 for 1 mile to Kings View Road. Turn right (W) onto King's View Road and go past the Devil's Canyon sign. Park before Pollock Bench at the Flume Canyon Trailhead. If there isn't room here, then go on and park at Pollock Bench.

Trail Description: Mostly horseback riders use Flume Creek Canyon, but it is a gorgeous 5 miles journey on foot as well. It is a diverse trail looping below the Pollock Bench trail, then up a plateau and down into Flume Creek Canyon. The Pollock Bench Trail and Devil's Canyon Overlook join Flume Creek along the way. To mark the trail, and distinguish it from other trails in the area, signs marked with F1, for Flume Creek Canyon, have been placed along the trail.

Mileage Estimate

0.0-0.5m Follow the trail below Pollock Bench and into the canyon to the loop junction.

0.5-2.5m Veer right (S) at the junction and follow the trail up onto the plateau. The partially hidden Pollock Bench trail can be found to the right (W).

2.5-3.3m Now the trail leads to the canyon wall, then turns left (N) and down into Flume Creek Canyon. Continue in the canyon wash. Devil's Canyon Overlook junction is to the right (SE), but it can be hard to locate.

3.3-4.5m Continue straight through the canyon until arriving at the beginning of the loop once again.

4.5-5.0m Make a right (N) here and follow it back to the parking lot and trailhead.

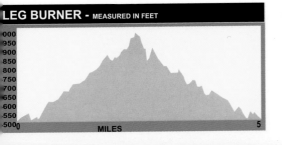

LEG BURNER - MEASURED IN FEET

(Elevation axis: 5000, 5050, 5100, 5150, 5200, 5250, 5300, 5350, 5400, 5450, 5500, 5550, 5600, 5650, 5700, 5750, 5800, 5850, 5900, 5950, 6000)

MILES 5

Pollock Bench - Black Ridge Canyons Wilderness (CCNCA)

Distance: 7.5 mile loop
Elevation Gain: 1900 feet
Foot Difficulty: Moderate

Use: Moderate-Heavy

Trail Location: Travel southwest out of Fruita on Highway 340 for 1 mile to King's View Road. Turn right (W) onto King's View Road and go past the Devil's Canyon sign. Park before Pollock Bench at the Flume Canyon Trailhead. If there isn't room here, then go on and park at Pollock Bench.

Mileage Estimate

0.0-0.5m Head out of the parking lot and up the DT to a trail gate.

0.5-1.0m There are some remarkable views of Flume Canyon up the slickrock section here.

1.0-1.8m Then go up a couple of rocky ridges to the trail junction. The loop starts here.

1.8-3.0m Veer left (S) and uphill on the trail.

3.0-5.4m Drop down to the right (N) toward the canyon, then left (E) to return on Flume Creek Canyon. Follow these few rocky areas along the bench and up to the Rattlesnake Arch junction on the left (N).

5.4-5.8m Turn right (S) and up to get out of the canyon and back to where the loop begins.

5.8-7.5m Turn left (NE), and descend to the parking lot.

Trail Description: Pollock Bench is a super day hike up stony benches and around the cliffs overlooking Pollock Canyon. The Flume Creek Canyon, Devil's Canyon, and Rattlesnake Arch trails can all be accessed from this trail as well. The P1 markers represent the trail for Pollock Bench. The BLM recently closed this trail to mountain biking.

LEG BURNER - MEASURED IN FEET

Distance: From 3 miles to 14 miles
Elevation Gain: 2,500 feet for the 14 mile loop   **Use:** Light
Foot Difficulty: Easy-Difficult

Trail Location: access 1 Just off Pollock Bench, see directions to Pollock Bench on page 75. Rattlesnake Arch begins 2.2 miles up Pollock Bench. This access involves the 13 mile out and back trip.

access 2 From the Colorado National Monument's west entrance, follow the road 11.5 miles. Turn right (W) at 16 Road/Glade Park. Just after the park boundary, take another right (NW) onto Black Ridge Road. Rattlesnake Arch access is 10 miles up the Upper or Lower Black Ridge Road. This 4x4 road is closed February 15 to April 15.

access 3 This entrance is by water via raft and requires launching from the Loma boat launch, then floating to the Rattlesnake Canyon base area.

West

Trail Description: Rattlesnake Arch is an outstanding trail that winds around numerous arches with endless canyon views. It is tough to access the complete loop, as it requires some climbing skills. There is a section of the loop where that requires some basic climbing skills for about 20 feet. The Pollock Bench access is the most difficult, with its own 8 foot section of rock that requires climbing. The 14 mile length of the Pollock Bench access is also a factor that makes it difficult. The Black Ridge Road access can be driven by a 4x4 vehicle or by a mountain bike. Just remember that Rattlesnake Arch is for hiking only. The access at the Colorado River has a hike through the canyon to the middle point of the loop. If you want to avoid all these climbing sections, then make sure you go north to start the trail from access 2. This route will double the miles, because you will have to backtrack out the same way. Whichever way you take, the views on this trail are so incredible that it is well worth the extra effort.

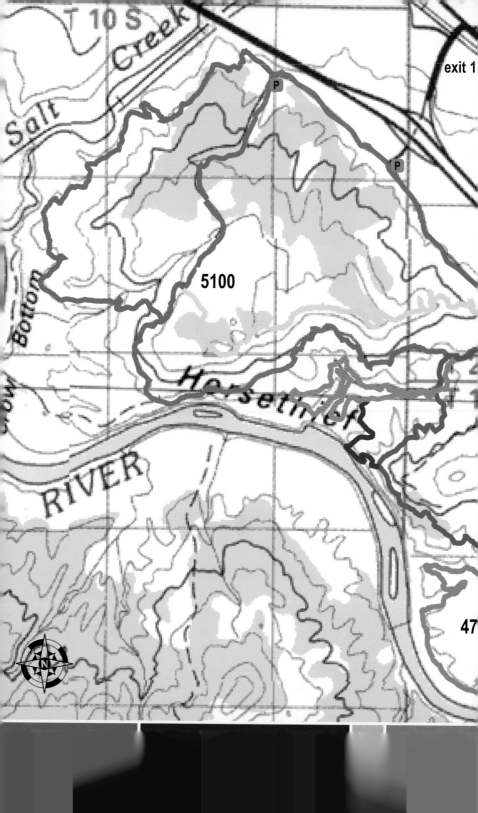

The Grand Loop - Kokopelli Trails (CCNCA)

Distance: 23.4 mile loop
Elevation Gain: 3,500 feet
Foot Difficulty: Moderate-Difficult
Use: Moderate-Heavy
Biking Difficulty: Moderate-Difficult

Trail Location: Drive west out of Grand Junction on I-70 to Loma Exit #15. Turn left (SW) and over I-70, then make a right (NW) turn at the sign that points to the Kokopelli Trail. Then turn left (SW) before the truck weigh station and over the cattle guard to the parking area with the bathrooms and trail information.

West

Mileage Estimate

0.0-0.6m Go up and over on the road to the Mary's Loop Trailhead sign.

0.6-2.0m Turn right (SW) and begin climbing up the sandstone ridge, making your way to Horsethief Bench.

2.0-6.0m Drop onto the trail, veering left (W) on the ST along Horsethief Bench over the Colorado River. Weave in and out of a canyon and a dry wash then climb out.

6.0-8.5m Turn left (N), and continue on Mary's Loop as it becomes a ST and then travels through some difficult areas to negotiate.

8.5-9.2m Turn left (W) onto Steve's Cutoff and then downhill along the ridge to the crack in the rock.

9.2-11.6m Make a hard left (W) at the crack. Continue along the ridge where the trail veers right (N) and uphill, joining a DT road.

11.6-13.9m Turn left (N) to Lion's Loop. Make another left (W) at the sign and box. From here, the trail becomes narrow and rocky with some technical sections.

13.9-14.5m Turn right (N) at the trail junction and climb to Troy Built.

14.5-18.5m Turn left (N) and go down into a small canyon wash then up and over along the northwestern ridge along the Salt Creek. Stay straight at the Kokopelli Trail junction and continue this technical ST to the DT.

18.5-23.4m Follow the main service road back to the parking.

Trail Description: The Grand Loop is known worldwide as a long loop encompassing 5 out of the 8 trails in the Kokopelli Trail System. It is a monster 23 mile loop makes its way from Horsethief Canyon, to the edge of Ruby Canyon and Salt Creek and then back. Add Mack Ridge and/or Moore Fun on the way back. This desert trail high above the Colorado River is especially busy in the spring and summer.

LEG BURNER - MEASURED IN FEET

5000	
4950	
4900	
4850	
4800	
4750	
4700	
4650	
4600	
4550	

Horsethief Bench - Kokopelli Trails (CCNCA)

Distance: 4.0 mile loop
Elevation Gain: 800 feet
Foot Difficulty: Easy-Moderate

Use: Moderate-Heavy
Biking Difficulty: Easy-Moderate

Trail Location: Drive west out of Grand Junction on I-70 to Loma Exit #15. Turn left (SW) and over I-70, then make a right (NW) turn at the sign that points to the Kokopelli Trail. Then turn left (SW) before the truck weigh station and over the cattle guard to the parking area with the bathrooms and trail information. Horsethief Bench is 2 miles from the parking lot by way of Mary's Loop.

West

Mileage Estimate

0.0-1.7m Descend a steep technical hill after crossing the cattle guard. At the base, turn left (S) and follow the rock wall toward the Colorado River. This trail will drop you into a wash and then out along the ridge.

1.7-2.9m Turn right (E) into a small canyon where you'll have to climb a few ledges then up and out on the top of the ridge.

2.9-3.8m Then go down into a winding dry wash below the sandstone cliff walls and back to the top of the ridge.

3.8-4.0m Turn left (E) and then climb out of Horsethief Bench. From here, continue Mary's Loop either to the left (N) or right (E).

Trail Description: Horsethief Bench is a loop along the Colorado River and is accessed from Mary's Loop. It treks through slickrock, some dry washes, and even a small canyon on the way below beautiful sandstone walls. This is a good trail anytime and any season.

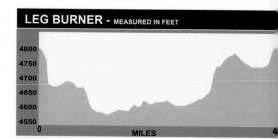

LEG BURNER - MEASURED IN FEET

4800
4750
4700
4650
4600
4550

0   MILES   4

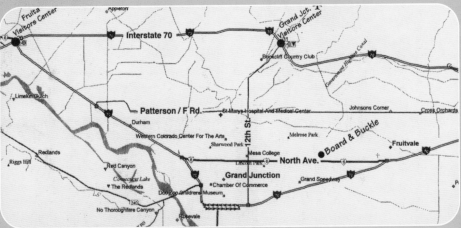

Lion's Loop - Kokopelli Trails (CCNCA)

Distance: 7.5 mile loop
Elevation Gain: 1,250 feet
Foot Difficulty: Easy-Moderate

Use: Moderate-Heavy
Biking Difficulty: Moderate-Difficult

Trail Location: Drive west out of Grand Junction on I-70 to Mack Exit #11. Turn left (SW) and then under I-70. This road will take you straight up to Mack Ridge Parking Lot.

West

Mileage Estimate

0.0-1.2m Go southeast from the parking area over the main service road.

1.2-1.4m Turn right (S) up the hill to the register box and map board.

1.4-1.8m Follow the DT downhill to the trail junction. Mary's Loop is to the left (S), Steve's is straight down, and Lion's Loop is on the right (W) and up.

1.8-3.9m Follow it up the ST where it becomes more rocky and technical.

3.9-4.5m Turn right (N) at the junction on the steep and rocky DT then up to the Troy Built junction.

4.5-5.7m Stay straight and continue along this rocky DT. As the trail levels off, go left (N) on Mack Ridge Road to the slow climb and leading to the steep downhill section.

5.7-6.5m Follow this steep downhill to the service road.

6.5-7.5m Make a right (E) and then follow the main service road back to the parking area.

Trail Description: Lion's Loop is a combination DT and ST that circles above the Colorado River. There are substantial technical spots and aerobic hills, so be extra careful in these spots. Mix and match Lion's Loop with any or all of the other Kokopelli Trails to add more miles to your outing. See the Kokopelli Trails map on page 77.

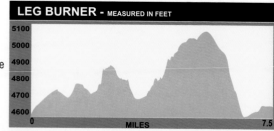

LEG BURNER - MEASURED IN FEET

5100
5000
4900
4800
4700
4600

0   MILES   7.5

Mack Ridge - Kokopelli Trails (CCNCA)

Distance: 7 miles one way
Elevation Gain: 925 feet
Foot Difficulty: Moderate

Use: Moderate-Heavy
Biking Difficulty: Moderate-Difficult

Trail Location: Drive west out of Grand Junction on I-70 to Mack Exit #11. Turn left (SW) and then under I-70. This road will take you straight up to the Mack Ridge Parking Lot

West

Trail Description: Mack Ridge is an extremely challenging technical trail for mountain bikers because it is narrow and slopes toward a cliff. There are many boulders that you will have to get over. It travels along the highest ridge in this desert grassland area and through scattered juniper trees overlooking the Colorado.

Mileage Estimate

0.0-1.2m Leave the Mack exit parking area to the southeast and follow the main service road to the Mary's/Lion's Loop and the Mack Ridge/Moore Fun access road.

1.2-1.4m Turn right (S) up the access road to the Mack Ridge Trailhead and the register box and map. Mack Ridge is on the right (NW).

1.4-4.0m Make a right (NW) atop the ridge onto the trail that overlooks Lion's Loop, Steve's Loop, and Horsethief Canyon. There are technical difficulties ahead as the trail eventually levels off and becomes a DT to the radio towers. Now the DT becomes an ST.

4.0-4.5m Follow along the ridge to the DT, and then to the Mack Ridge Road and Lion's Loop.

4.5-7.0m A fun option at this point is to take Lion's or Troy Built. Or take a right (N) on Mack Ridge Road to the parking area.

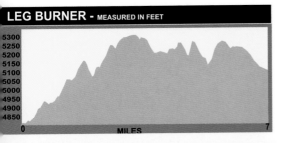

LEG BURNER - MEASURED IN FEET

Mary's Loop - Kokopelli Trails (CCNCA)

Distance: 8.5 mile loop
Elevation Gain: 1,125 feet
Foot Difficulty: Easy-Moderate

Use: Heavy
Biking Difficulty: Easy-Moderate

Trail Location: Drive west out of Grand Junction on I-70 to Loma Exit #15. Turn left (SW) and over I-70, then make a right (NW) turn at the sign that heads to the Kokopelli Trail. Then turn left (SW) before the truck weigh station and over the cattle guard to the parking area with the bathrooms and trail information.

Mileage Estimate

0.0-0.6m Go directly up the dirt road and over the hogback. Then go back down the road and look for the trailhead.

0.6-2.0m Make a sharp right (SW) and follow the DT up the sandstone ridge to the Horsethief Bench Trailhead on the left (W) where the register box is located.

2.0-4.5m Veer right (N) and follow the ridge. It will become a ST with some moderate ups, downs and technical spots. The majority of this section is ST but will become DT at the Steve's Cutoff intersections.

4.5-6.0m Take the DT 1.5 miles straight past the Lion's Loop intersection and up to the top of the hill and the Moore Fun/Mack Ridge Trailheads.

6.0-8.5m Head down the hill and turn right (SE) onto the main service road to the parking area.

Trail Description: Mary's Loop is the most popular loop of the world renowned Kokopelli Trails. It is heavily traveled by mountain bikers and hikers from all over the world. There are a few places that can be challenging and are narrow enough to warrant extra caution. Add Horsethief Bench and/or Steve's Loop if there is time. The wonderful views of the Colorado River, Horsethief Canyon, and the Uncompahgre Plateau can by enjoyed even more during the week when the trail is less crowded. Whatever day you choose, Mary's Loop makes one marvelous adventure.

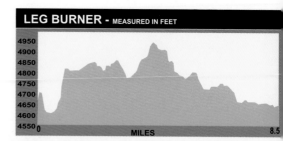

LEG BURNER - MEASURED IN FEET

4950 4900 4850 4800 4750 4700 4650 4600 4550

0   MILES   8.5

85

Moore Fun - Kokopelli Trails (CCNCA)

Distance: 4.8 miles one-way/ 7.5 miles via service road
Elevation Gain: 1,025 feet   **Use:** Light
Foot Difficulty: Moderate   **Biking Difficulty:** Difficult

Trail Location: Drive west out of Grand Junction on I-70 to Loma Exit #15. Turn left (SW) and over I-70, then make a right (NW) turn at the sign that points to the Kokopelli Trail. Then turn left (SW) before the truck weigh station and over the cattle guard to the parking area with the bathrooms and trail information.

Mileage Estimate

0.0-0.4m   Go directly up the dirt road and over the hogback. Then go back down the road and look for the trailhead.

0.4-2.0m   Turn right (NW) and follow the trail across a DT road and up a very technical section. At the top, in an open valley, look northwest for the trail that continues up the ridge.

2.0-3.0m   Struggle up this ridge overlooking the Colorado River and Mary's Loop.

3.0-4.8m   Cross the top of the ridge to the west, then down to the technical trail. This section overlooks Lion's Loop, and Steve's Loop on the way to the register box and the map.

4.8-7.5m   Continue onto any one of the other 4 Kokopelli Trails accessible from this point or go down the ST to the main service road and back to the parking area.

Trail Description: Moore Fun is the newest and most technically difficult trail in the Kokopelli Loops Trail System. At the end, you can choose from four different trails to extend your pleasure: Mary's Loop, Lion's Loop, Mack Ridge or Steve's Loop. There are unique views of the desert out to the Book Cliffs.

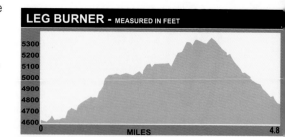

LEG BURNER - MEASURED IN FEET

5300
5200
5100
5000
4900
4800
4700
4600
0   MILES   4.8

Rustler's Loop - Kokopelli Trails (CCNCA)

Distance: 3.6 mile loop
Elevation Gain: 650 feet
Foot Difficulty: Easy

Use: Moderate-Heavy
Biking Difficulty: Easy

Trail Location: Drive west out of Grand Junction on I-70 to Loma Exit #15. Turn left (SW) and over I-70, then make a right (NW) turn at the sign that points to the Kokopelli Trail. Then turn left (SW) before the truck weigh station and over the cattle guard and past the parking area with the bathrooms and trail information. Drive on the dirt road up and over the ridge and down just past Mary's Loop. Park here.

West

Mileage Estimate

0.0-0.8m Go through the gate to the large map and the start of the trail. Veer right (W) and head west along the base of the rock wall.

0.8-2.3m At the plateau that overlooks the Colorado River, cross the private property by way of the rancher's access road and continue southeast, traveling next to the river.

2.3-3.6m After the short uphill switchback, the trail starts back toward the beginning of the loop and the parking lot.

Trail Description: Rustler's Loop is an easy trail with instruction on mountain biking and information on the natural environment in the area. It is an easy trail that is just right for those who are learning the proper mountain biking skills or for a low impact run. And at the downhill DT, there is the unique sight of a home cut right out of the sandstone wall. Please respect the private property that is along and nearby this trail.

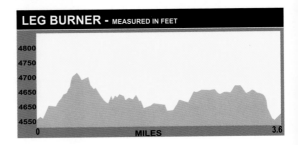

LEG BURNER - MEASURED IN FEET

Steve's Loop & Steve's Cut off - Kokopelli Trails (CCNCA)

Distance: 6.8 mile loop
Elevation Gain: 1,100 feet
Foot Difficulty: Easy-Moderate

Use: Moderate-Heavy
Biking Difficulty: Moderate

Trail Location: To get to Steve's Loop, drive west out of Grand Junction on I-70 to Mack Exit #11. Turn left (SW) and then under I-70 to the Mack Ridge Parking Lot.

Distance: 0.7 mile one way
Elevation Gain: feet
Foot Difficulty: Easy-Moderate

Use: Moderate-Heavy
Biking Difficulty: Moderate

Trail Location: Steve's Cutoff begins between Steve's Loop at 2.5 miles and along Mary's Loop at 4.5 miles.

Mileage Estimate (Steve's Loop)

0.0-1.2m Begin southeast along the main service road.

1.2-1.4m Turn right (S) and up the hill to the register box and map board.

1.4-1.8m Follow the DT downhill to the three way trail junction.

1.8-2.0m Steve's Loop begins here on a narrow ST between Lion's Loop and Mary's Loop.

2.0-2.4m Cross the road and down a difficult section into the wash. At the crack in the rock, veer right (W). Steve's Cutoff heads off to the left (S).

2.4-3.6m Travel along the ridge, back into a canyon and then out along the technical section.

3.6-4.8m As you enter a dry wash, the trail veers uphill to the right (N). It levels out and becomes a DT.

4.8-5.0m Turn left (N) up the narrow ST to where Steve's Loop began.

5.0-5.4m Veer right (N), then up and over the hill.

5.4-6.8m Turn left (NW) on the main service road to parking.

Trail Description: Steve's Loop hugs the ridge most of the way as it travels below and between Mary's Loop and Lion's Loop. It has some amazing views of the Colorado River and is therefore worth it to make it the sole trail on a trip or use it for more miles after Mary's Loop or Lion's Loop. Steve's Cutoff connects Mary's Loop and Steve's Loop.

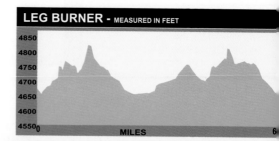

LEG BURNER - MEASURED IN FEET

4850
4800
4750
4700
4650
4600
4550

MILES

Troy Built Loop - Kokopelli Trails (CCNCA)

Distance: 8 mile loop
Elevation Gain: 1,150feet
Foot Difficulty: Moderate

Use: Moderate-Heavy
Biking Difficulty: Moderate-Difficult

Trail Location: Drive west out of Grand Junction on I-70 to Mack Exit #11. Turn left (SW) and then under I-70. This road will take you straight up to the Mack Ridge Parking Lot.

West

Mileage Estimate

0.0-1.2m From the Mack Ridge Parking Lot, follow the service road northwest to the trailhead and the ST.

1.2-2.6m Take the ST downhill and into a slickrock wash, around a ridge, up and then down to the Troy Built Loop and the Kokopelli junction.

2.6-3.6m Veer left (SW) along the ridgeline ST above Salt Creek Canyon and the Colorado River.

3.6-5.2m Go down into a wash/canyon, then back out and up on a rocky ST to the Lion's/Troy Built junction.

5.2-6.2m Turn left (N) up the rocky DT and stay left (N) on Mack Ridge Road to the downhill.

6.2-7.0m Follow this steep downhill to the main service road.

7.0-8.0m Make a right (E) on the main service road and follow it back to the parking area.

Trail Description: Troy Built is a combination DT and ST that takes you along Salt Creek Canyon and above the Colorado River and Ruby Canyon area. The tight ST section along the ridge is a little unstable at times due to the steep exposure. It offers splendid views of the north tip of the Uncompahgre Plateau.

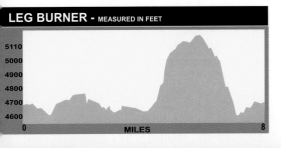

LEG BURNER - MEASURED IN FEET

5110	
5000	
4900	
4800	
4700	
4600	
0	MILES	8

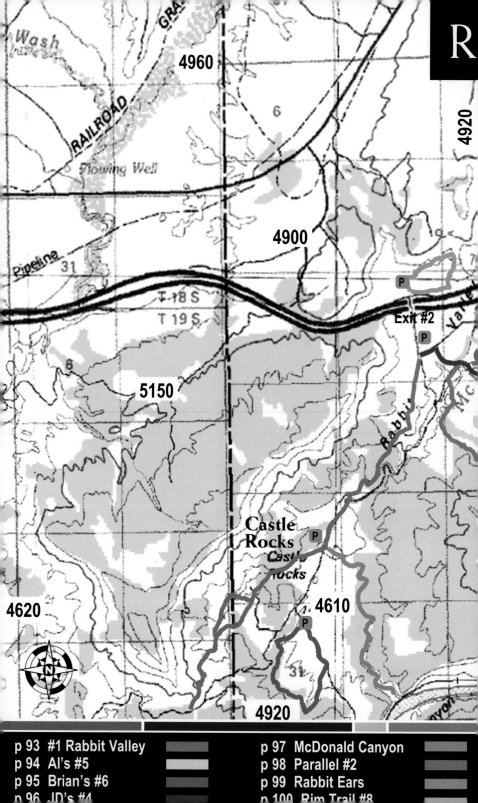

R

Wash

RAILROAD

GRA...

4960

6

Flowing Well

4920

Pipeline 31

4900

T 18 S

T 19 S

P

Exit #2

6

5150

Rabb...

Mc...

Va...

Castle
Rocks

Castle
Rocks

P

4610

P

4620

N

3...

4920

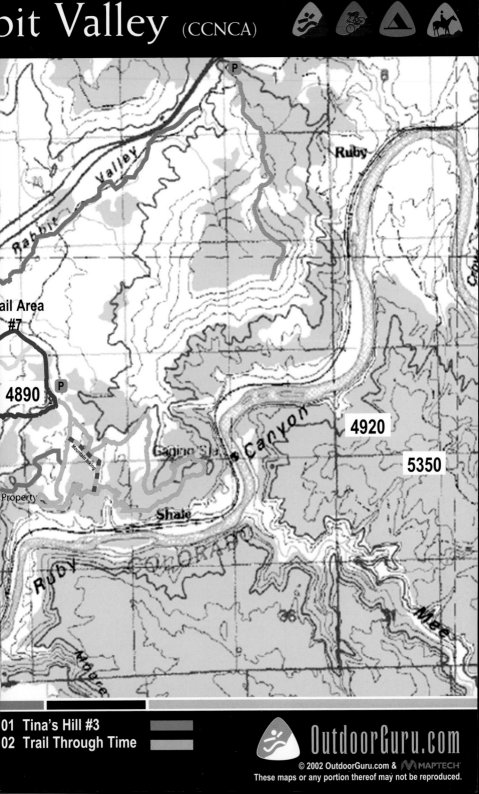

bit Valley (CCNCA)

4890   P

Ruby

Trail Area
#7

Canyon

4920

5350

Ganino's

Property

Shale

Ruby   COLORADO

Mee

Moore

OutdoorGuru.com

#1-Rabbit Valley (CCNCA)

Distance: 3 miles one way/ 6 miles out and back
Elevation Gain: 550 feet   **Use:** Moderate
Foot Difficulty: Moderate   **Biking Difficulty:** Moderate

Trail Location: 25 miles out of Grand Junction west on Interstate 70. Exit at Rabbit Valley Exit #2 on the south side of I-70 where the road turns into dirt. Follow the dirt road to the first left(E) and make another quick left(N) into a large parking area with bathrooms. Trail #1 begins at Trail Area #7, 1 mile southeast of the parking lot. See Rabbit Valley Trails map on page 91.

West

LEG BURNER - MEASURED IN FEET

Mileage Estimate

0.0-3.0m   This is a narrow ST through the Macdonald Wash and alongside the Kokopelli Trail. Then it connects with Al's #5.

3.0-6.0m   The trail ends where the Kokopelli Trail begins a steep uphill climb. Turn around and follow the trail or the Kokopelli Trail back.

Trail Description: Rabbit Valley Trail #1 is a popular horseback riding trail running east next to the Kokopelli Trail. It is sandy and rocky as it goes through the wash and becomes a narrow ST along the road. Rabbit Ears and its parking area is just a short distance up the hill from the end of this trail.

Al's #5 - Rabbit Valley (CCNCA)

Distance: 2.3 miles one way/ 4.6 miles out and back
Elevation Gain: 325 feet/300 feet   **Use:** Moderate
Foot Difficulty: Easy   **Biking Difficulty:** Easy

Trail Location: 25 miles out of Grand Junction west on I-70. Exit at Rabbit Valley Exit #2 on the south side of I-70 where the road turns into dirt. Follow the dirt road to the first left (E) and make another quick left (N) into a large parking area with bathrooms. Al's #5 starts southeast of Trail Area #7, 1 mile from the parking area.

Mileage Estimate

0.0-0.3m Leave the parking area to the left (NE) and over a cattle guard. Turn right (S) to Trail Area #7.

0.3-0.8m Veer left (NE) and travel along the road as you approach Trail Area #7.

0.8-1.2m Turn right (SE) at the #5 trail sign and travel southeast across the JD's #4 junction.

1.2-2.3m Continue southeast through a small canyon to another junction with JD's #4.

2.3-4.6m The trail ends here where it meets JD's #4. Turn around or continue on JD's #4.

Trail Description: Al's #5 connects #1 and JD's #4. It crosses JD's #4 once and then meets it again at the end of the trail. It is a short trek through this desert valley area.

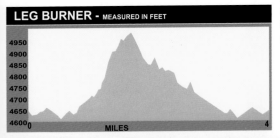

LEG BURNER - MEASURED IN FEET

4950
4900
4850
4800
4750
4700
4650
4600
0   MILES   4

94

Brian's #6 - Rabbit Valley (CCNCA)

Distance: 3.2 mile loop
Elevation Gain: 325 feet
Foot Difficulty: Easy

Use: Moderate
Biking Difficulty: Easy-Moderate

Trail Location: 25 miles out of Grand Junction on I-70. Exit at Rabbit Valley Exit #2 on the south side of I-70 where the road turns into dirt. Follow the dirt road to the first parking lot to the left (E). You can park here and walk or ride 3 miles up Kokopelli Trail to to the start of Brian's #6. If you wish to drive this distance, it is recommended to have a 4x4 high clearance vehicle. If driving, take the Kokopelli southwest, past the Castle Rocks to a left at the road heading to the Knowles Canyon Overlook campsite. Follow this road for 0.25 miles to the dam. The trail begins to the west of the dam. See Rabbit Valley map on page 91.

West

Mileage Estimate

0.0-0.5m Go southwest from the dam to the junction with Brian's #6.

0.5-2.2m Make a left (S) turn off the DT and follow the trail signs along the slickrock. The trail changes from slickrock to some loose and steep ups and downs through the canyon wash to the road to the Knowles Canyon Overlook campsite.

2.2-3.2m Make a left (NW) onto this road and follow it back to where you parked.

Trail Description: Brian's #5 works its way out along some slickrock, then up and down along the ridgeline with some beautiful views of the sandstone walls and some rock features. This trail makes and excellent loop combined with Kokopelli and Parallel #2.

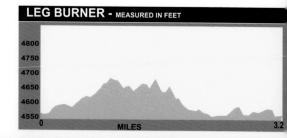

LEG BURNER - MEASURED IN FEET

4800	
4750	
4700	
4650	
4600	
4550	

0   MILES   3.2

JD's #4 - Rabbit Valley (CCNCA)

Distance: 5 mile loop
Elevation Gain: 700 feet
Foot Difficulty: Easy-Moderate

Use: Moderate
Biking Difficulty: Moderate

Trail Location: 25 miles out of Grand Junction on I-70. Exit at Rabbit Valley Exit #2 on the south side of I-70 where the road turns into dirt. Follow the dirt road to the first left (E) and make another quick left (N) into a large parking area with bathrooms. JD's #4 starts southeast of Trail Area #7, 1 mile from the parking area.

Mileage Estimate

0.0-0.3m Turn left (NE) out of the parking lot and then go right (S) after the cattle guard.

0.3-0.8m Stay straight as you approach Trail Area #7.

0.8-1.2m Continue west out of Trail Area #7 and veer right (SE) at the start of the loop and the #4 trail sign. Continue uphill, going south.

1.2-2.0m At the top, drop down a steep hill to the left (E) and the Rim Trail #8 junction.

2.0-2.3m Turn left (N), and follow the trail downhill to the north on the rough, rocky road.

2.3-3.0m Make another left (NW), jumping back on the ST. Follow this past the Al's #5 junction.

3.0-3.8m The trail veers left (W) and arrives once again at the start of the loop and Trail Area #7.

3.8-5.0m Continue through Trail Area #7 to the parking lot.

Trail Description: JD's #4 travels along a good ST through the desert valley and to a ridge overlooking the Colorado River and Rim Trail #8. It has access to Al's #5 and Rim Trail #8 for extended miles.

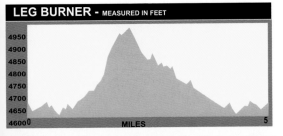

LEG BURNER - MEASURED IN FEET

4950
4900
4850
4800
4750
4700
4650
4600

0

MILES

5

McDonald Canyon - Rabbit Valley (CCNCA)

Distance: 2.1 miles one way/ 4.2 miles out and back
Elevation Gain: 200 feet   **Use:** Light
Foot Difficulty: Easy

Trail Location: 25 miles out of Grand Junction on I-70. Exit at Rabbit Valley Exit #2 on the south side of I-70 where the road turns into dirt. Follow the dirt road to the first parking lot on the left (E). You can park here and walk or ride to the beginning of McDonald Canyon 2.5 miles on the Kokopelli Trail. If you wish to drive to the trailhead, continue southwest on the Kokopelli Trail and park in the lot on the left (S). It is recommended to have a 4x4 or 4x2 high clearance vehicle to drive to McDonald Canyon.

Mileage Estimate

0.0-0.6m Begin this trail down in the creek bed southeast from the parking lot. It then makes its way in and out of the this creek bed between the canyon walls.

0.6-0.8m The trail slides down a few ledges on the left (E) hand side of the creek bed and then into the base of the canyon. Here you can turn right (N) and head back to the bottom of the waterfall to view some pictographs and petroglyphs on both sides of the canyon walls.

0.8-1.6m The trail continues further south into the canyon along the rocky creek bed for another mile to a trail on the left (SE).

1.6-2.1m Look and turn left (E) as you approach the cottonwood trees and follow the trail on the left (NE) of the canyon. Reach the largest alcove near the mouth of the creek and the last rock art panel.

2.1-4.2m Turn around at the railroad tracks where the trail ends.

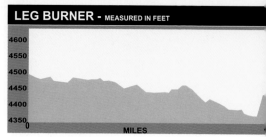

LEG BURNER - MEASURED IN FEET

4600
4550
4500
4450
4400
4350
0

MILES

Trail Description: McDonald Canyon runs along a dry creek bed, which usually has standing water after rainstorms and snowmelt. It doesn't have significant elevation changes, but does have many examples of ancient rock art such as pictographs and petrogylphs. The pictographs are drawings or paintings of animals, people, or intricate designs. The petroglyphs depict the same subjects, but they are etched, scratched or otherwise carved out of the rock. To protect these irreplaceable images, please do not scale the walls for a closer look or touch them. If you get lost anywhere along the trail, just follow the creek bed out to the railroad tracks and the Colorado River.

Parallel #2 - Rabbit Valley (CCNCA)

Distance: 5.2 miles one way/ 10.4 miles out and back
Elevation Gain: 1,000 feet/850 feet   **Use:** Moderate-Heavy
Foot Difficulty: Moderate   **Biking Difficulty:** Moderate

Trail Location: 25 miles out of Grand Junction west on I-70. Exit at Rabbit Valley Exit #2 on the south side of I-70 where the road turns into dirt. Follow the dirt road to the first left (E) and make another quick left (N) into a large parking area with bathrooms.

Mileage Estimate

0.0-2.5m Leave the parking area to the right (S) and follow the Parallel #2 signs. Then it drops in elevation as you get closer to the Castle Rock landmark.

2.5-3.5m Follow the Kokopelli Trail Road to two sets of bathrooms. Remain on the straight path and then turn right (W), following the Parallel #2 sign to the fork in the trail.

Trail Description: Parallel #2 is a 10 mile ST/DT that weaves in and out and alongside the Kokopelli Trail. Just follow the trail signs and cairns, but be careful not to go too far if you've planned for the 10 mile out and back. There are several sandstone rock formations such as the Castle Rocks that can be viewed from a distance from this trail. The trail ends at the Kokopelli Trail Road just east of the Utah border at the start of the Western Rim.

3.5-5.2m Go right (W) as the trail works its way down and around a mountain. Stay on the ST until it meets the Kokopelli Trail.

5.2-10.4m Turn around or cross the Kokopelli Trail Road to the sandy Western Rim.

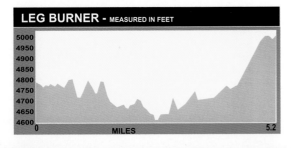

LEG BURNER - MEASURED IN FEET

Rabbit Ears - Rabbit Valley (CCNCA)

Distance: 2.5 miles one way/ 5 miles out and back
Elevation Gain: 950 feet   **Use:** Moderate
Foot Difficulty: Moderate

Trail Location: 25 miles out of Grand Junction on I-70. Exit at Rabbit Valley Exit #2 on the south side of I-70 where the road turns into dirt. Follow the dirt road to the first left (E). Follow the Kokopelli Trail for 4.4 miles to the trailhead and park in the Rabbit Ears parking lot on the right (SE). Watch out for the large and sandy potholes.

West

Mileage Estimate

0.0-1.0m   The trail is out through the trees and over some slickrock, on the way up the ridge to a large open crack in the cliff.

1.0-2.0m   On the other side of the crack and along an exposed ridge overlooking Ruby Canyon the trail will have some short and steep uphills with loose dirt and rocks.

2.0-2.5m   The last half mile levels off atop the plateau. It stops suddenly at the edge of a ridge overlooking the Colorado River.

2.5-5.0m   Turn around and head back the way you came.

Trail Description: Rabbit Ears has great panoramic views of Utah, the Book Cliffs, and Grand junction as it follows atop a ridge and through the crack between the 20 foot high rock walls. It is a moderate hike to the top where it stops at the edge of a ridge. Don't be surprised to see a rabbit or two along the way.

LEG BURNER - MEASURED IN FEET

5700	
5600	
5500	
5400	
5300	
5200	
5100	

0   MILES   2

Rim Trail #8 - Rabbit Valley (CCNCA)

Distance: 7.5 miles
Elevation Gain: 1,550 feet
Foot Difficulty: Moderate

Use: Moderate
Biking Difficulty: Moderate-Difficult

Trail Location: access 1 25 miles out of Grand Junction on I-70. Exit at Rabbit Valley Exit #2 on the south side of I-70 where the road turns into dirt. Follow the dirt road to the first left (E) and make another quick left (N) into a large parking area with bathrooms. Travel on Tina's Hill #3 for 3.7 miles to where it meets Rim Trail #8. Or travel JD's #4 for 2.2 miles to where it meets the beginning Rim Trail #8.
access 2 Take the Kokopelli Trail east around 2 miles past the parking area. Turn right (SE) next to the corral and follow this dirt road south to the ridge and JD's #4. Park here.

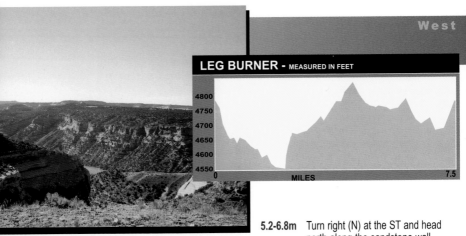

West

LEG BURNER - MEASURED IN FEET

4800
4750
4700
4650
4600
4550

0   MILES   7.5

Mileage Estimate (starting from access 1)

0.0-0.2m From the top of JD's #4 travel down a steep and rocky DT.

0.2-1.2m Follow this DT south past Tina's Hill #3 on the right (NW). Continue down the sandy trail until reaching the rim overlooking the Colorado River.

1.2-2.7m The trail veers left (E) and follows a ST along and over some ledges and through a rocky technical area.

2.7-4.8m Stay straight (E) or veer left (N) here. It is strongly recommended that mountain bikers do not go straight because the trail becomes too sandy and difficult to peddle.

4.8-5.2m Continue on the straight (E) path to the east along the rim overlooking the Colorado River. Soon the trail will turn back west where the DT and ST come together at the corner of the sandstone wall.

5.2-6.8m Turn right (N) at the ST and head north along the sandstone wall. There are steep, sandy ups and downs through a cove and then west to the next junction.

6.8-7.5m At this junction, take a hard right (N) or stay straight (NW). The steep, sandy ups and downs continue on the path to the right. It is suggested that mountain bikers veer left (NW) to continue the easier, less sandy route to the ridge.

Trail Description: Rim #8 can be soft and sandy at times, which can make it difficult to trek along. However, there are such wonderful views along the river and the ridge wall that it makes it well worth the struggle.

Tina's Hill #3 - Rabbit Valley (CCNCA)

Distance: 3.7 miles one way/ 7.4 miles out and back
Elevation Gain: 750 feet/700 feet   **Use:** Moderate
Foot Difficulty: Easy-Moderate   **Biking Difficulty:** Moderate

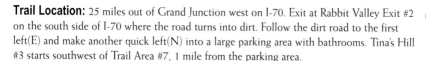

Trail Location: 25 miles out of Grand Junction west on I-70. Exit at Rabbit Valley Exit #2 on the south side of I-70 where the road turns into dirt. Follow the dirt road to the first left(E) and make another quick left(N) into a large parking area with bathrooms. Tina's Hill #3 starts southwest of Trail Area #7, 1 mile from the parking area.

West

Mileage Estimate

0.0-1.5m Leave the parking lot to the left (E) and over the cattle guard. Make a quick right (S) and follow the trail a short distance, veering right (SW) at the Trail #3 sign. Now it follows along the fence line on a good ST.

1.5-2.24m Trek up a couple of steep hills where the trail gets rockier and arrives at a private property sign. Please respect the private property.

2.4-3.7m Here the trail has a few technical exposed ridges, then drops into a very soft and sandy area on the way to the Rim Trail #8 junction.

3.7-7.4m Continue right (S) or left (N) on Rim Trail #8 or turn around to complete the out and back.

Trail Description: Tina's Hill works its way up atop the ridge overlooking the Colorado River and Rabbit Valley. The part of this trail travels across private property, so please be respectful. For an extended trip, get on Rim Trail #8 and go to JD's #4 and Al's #5.

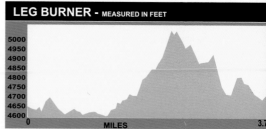

LEG BURNER - MEASURED IN FEET

5000
4950
4900
4850
4800
4750
4700
4650
4600

0   MILES   3.7

Trail Through Time - Rabbit Valley (CCNCA)

Distance: 1.5 miles out and back
Elevation Gain: 150 feet
Foot Difficulty: Easy

Use: Moderate

Trail Location: 25 miles out of Grand Junction on I-70. Exit at Rabbit Valley Exit #2 on the north side of I-70 where the road turns into dirt. Park here.

West

Trail Description: Trail Through Time is an interpretive trail that travels through the desert valley and educates travelers by numbering and explaining some points of interest along the trail. The points of interest include fossils, plant life, or geological objects. For example, there are the Camarasaurus and the unidentified dinosaur fossils. Fossilized twigs, branches, leaves and insects offer other prehistoric viewing opportunities. There is also information about the surrounding rock features and the geologic processes that have created them. Many forms of wildlife can be seen, such as coyotes, rabbits, bats, squirrels, golden eagles and an occasional bald eagle in the winter months. Pinyon pines, junipers, prickly pear cacti, wildflowers, and yucca plants are some of the plant life that can be enjoyed from this trail. There are also 3 species of rattlesnakes in the area, so watch out for these and be prepared for a poisonous encounter by carrying a snake bite kit.

Mileage Estimate
0.0-1.5m Up to a quarry and the billboard with educational information. The trail does a short loop along a ridge and back out to the dirt road and parking area.

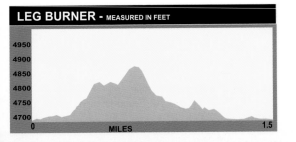

LEG BURNER - MEASURED IN FEET

4950	
4900	
4850	
4800	
4750	
4700	
0	MILES	1.5

YOUR BASE CAMP FOR OUTDOOR ADVENTURE

The newly remodeled Adam's Mark Grand Junction features:

273 Guest Rooms and 14 Spacious Suites

State of the Art Fitness Center

Swimming Pool & Jacuzzi

3 Outdoor, Lighted Tennis Courts

Over 12,000 sq. ft of Banquet and

Meeting Space with Full Service Catering

Casually Elegant, open-air restaurant featuring local cuisine for the whole family.

Sports Lounge

A lively sports bar with all the sports action on two 8 foot video walls. Don't just be a fan, be a player at PLAYERS!

970-241-8888
743 Horizon Drive
Grand Junction, CO 81506

*T*he Book Cliffs trail systems are hard to beat and encompass a staggering array of first-rate trails off of 16, 18, 21 and 25 Roads. Book Cliff trails are revered by any Coloradoan who has flown down and peddled up Chutes and Ladders, hiked Mount Garfield, or enjoyed the panoramic views from the Edge Loop. An area highlight is the low elevation of 4,500 to 6,000 feet, allowing year-round enjoyment—even in the depths of winter. Watch out for passing rain storms, which can turn the trails into masses of glue-like mud. The sagebrush shrubland, pinyon and juniper woodland are home to hundreds of wild horses (frequent visitors to the north of Mount Garfield), elusive western rattlesnakes, pronghorn antelope, golden eagles and the ever-present coyote. The Book Cliffs exemplify the Grand Valley's immense scope through massive climbs and lengthy interconnecting trails.

Magnetic Pole or North Pole

Compasses point to the magnetic pole so it is necessary to take into consideration compass declination, the difference between the true north pole and the magnetic pole. Topographic maps show the declination in degrees either east or west from north.

Magnetic Pole or
North Pole

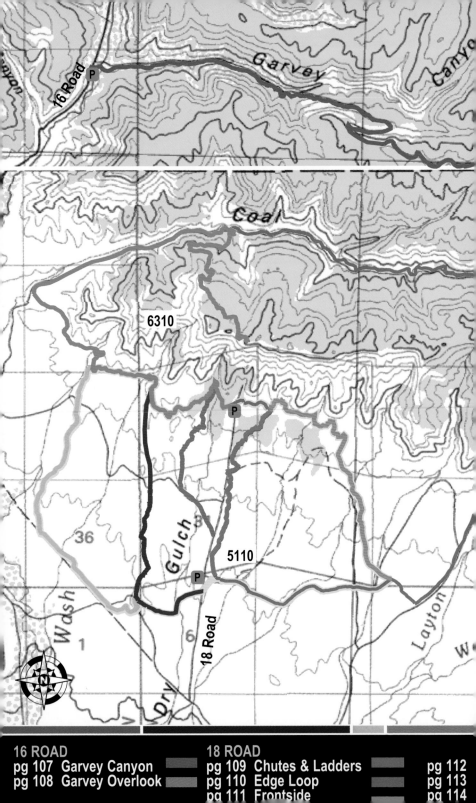

Fruita Area
16/18 Road

050

ılch

P

7070   Garfield
        Mesa

6560

36   Ross Ridge   31

7220

OutdoorGuru.com

© 2002 OutdoorGuru.com &   MAPTECH

These maps or any portion thereof may not be reproduced

Garvey Canyon - Book Cliffs/16 Road

Distance: 8.4 miles one way/ 16.8 out and back
Elevation Gain: 2,000 feet /1,000 feet   **Use:** Moderate
Foot Difficulty: Easy-Moderate   **Biking Difficulty** Easy-Moderate

Trail Location: Travel west out of Grand Junction on I-70 to Fruita Exit #19. Turn right (N) into Fruita to the stop sign and make a left (W) onto Aspen Street. Aspen Street merges into Hwy 6 & 50 to the northwest. Follow this road for 1.3 miles and turn right (N) onto 16 Road. Follow 16 Road for 17.5 miles to a right (E) and park at the Garvey Canyon Trailhead.

North

Mileage Estimate

0.0-3.0m Travel east and climb gently up the DT through the canyon.

3.0-6.3m The trail turns right (W) up to steep switchbacks as it makes its way to the top of a ridge. Continue northeast along this trail to the next trail junction.

6.3-8.4m Turn right (NE) and continue climbing to the top of the ridge and the Garvey Overlook junction.

8.4-16.8m Head back or continue along Garvey Overlook.

Trail Description: Garvey Canyon trail travels through the canyon that shares its name and then overlooks the canyon. It has incredible views of the Book Cliffs and the deep gulch shown in the picture above. Wildlife such as deer are visible from the smooth DT.

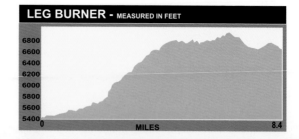

LEG BURNER - MEASURED IN FEET

Garvey Overlook - Book Cliffs/16 Road

Distance: 3.6 one way/ 7.2 out and back
Elevation Gain: 950 feet   **Use:** Moderate
Foot Difficulty: Easy-Moderate   **Biking Difficulty:** Moderate

Trail Location: Travel west out of Grand Junction on I-70 to Fruita Exit #19. Turn right (N) into Fruita to the stop sign and make a left (W) onto Aspen Street. Aspen Street merges into Hwy 6 & 50 to the northwest. Follow this road for 1.3 miles and turn right (N) onto 16 Road. Follow 16 Road for 13.8 miles and turn right (E) through a dry wash onto Coal Canyon Road. Follow Coal Canyon Road for 7.2 miles to the Garvey Overlook Trailhead on the left/north. Park alongside the road.

North

Mileage Estimate

0.0-1.9m Travel northeast in and out of the rocky dry wash to the first trail junction.

1.9-3.0m Turn left (W) up a DT road and through the canyon to the next trail junction.

3.0-3.2m Turn left (W) on the rugged DT uphill to where the faint trail continues left (S) .

3.2-3.6m Follow the ST south along the mountain edge, where it can be difficult to follow because it is a faint narrow ST. Continue to the trail end overlooking the back of the Book Cliffs.

Trail Description: Garvey Overlook goes through a picturesque canyon on the way to Garvey Canyon. The path through the canyon is a rocky yet gentle incline. It has amazing views of the Horsemountains to the north and some wildlife such as deer, elk and bear can also be seen.

3.6-7.2m Head back or continue through Garvey Canyon to the west after returning to the DT.

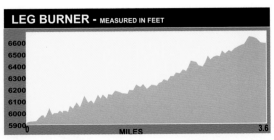

LEG BURNER - MEASURED IN FEET

Chutes and Ladders - Book Cliffs/18 Road

Distance: 4.6 miles one way/ 9.2 miles out and back
Elevation Gain: 950 feet   **Use:** Moderate-Heavy
Foot Difficulty: Easy-Moderate   **Biking Difficulty:** Easy-Difficult

Trail Location: From downtown Fruita, at the roundabout (Circle Park), go east on Aspen Street. Go 4 blocks to Maple Street, also known as 17 1/2 Road. Turn left (N). Drive 4 miles and turn right (E) on N 3/10 Road. Follow N 3/10 Road to the T intersection at 18 Road. Turn left (N) on 18 Road and follow it for 4.3 miles to the main parking area. Chutes and Ladders starts at the trail across the road, downhill to the pond, and east. Or make a left and travel 2.2 miles up Prime Cut to the start of the Chutes and Ladders.

North

Mileage Estimate

0.0-0.2m Start out of the main 18 Road parking lot. Cross the road and go down the ST to the dry pond.

0.2-1.8m Veer right (E) at the pond and continue on short ups and downs across the prairie to reach the corral.

1.8-3.9m Turn left (NW) at the corral. Follow the gentle incline up toward the cliffs.

3.9-4.6m Cross the dirt road. Here you will encounter steep hills on a tight ST. This is where the fun begins and the trail lives up to its name.

4.6-9.2m When you reach the Prime Cut junction, head back to complete the out and back. Or continue down Prime Cut, Frontside, Joe's Ridge, or Zippety Doo Daa.

Trail Description: The name of this trail says it all, describing perfectly the steep ups and steeper downs running along the base of the Book Cliffs. The only flat portion of this trail is the first 2 miles along the prairie. Due to these factors, Chutes and Ladders is only for those who are the most fit with a high level of endurance. Be cautious of the many cattle track ruts and of other trail users when descending.

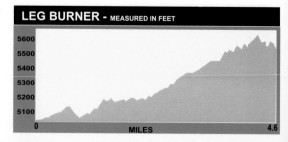

LEG BURNER - MEASURED IN FEET

MILES	
5600	
5500	
5400	
5300	
5200	
5100	
0 ... 4.6	

Edge Loop - Book Cliffs/18 Road

Distance: 28.6 mile loop
Elevation Gain: 4,500 + feet
Foot Difficulty: Easy-Difficult

Use: Moderate
Biking Difficulty: Moderate-Difficult

Trail Location: From downtown Fruita, at the roundabout (Circle Park), go east on Aspen Street. Go 4 blocks to Maple Street, also known as 17 1/2 Road. Turn left (N). Drive 4 miles and turn right (E) on N 3/10 Road. Follow N 3/10 Road to the T intersection at 18 Road. Turn left (N) on 18 Road and follow it for 4.3 miles to the main parking area. Edge Loop begins 2.2 miles along Prime Cut.

Trail Description: Edge Loop is an epic loop with some long and difficult sections but also some easy ones. It has awe inspiring views of the Book Cliffs, the Grand Valley, and the Horse Mountains. Just pick which view you like best and break up this long loop into more than one day by camping anywhere except near 18 Road.

11.4-15.7m Turn right (E) and continue up the very steep road to the top. Continue on to the Hunter Canyon junction.

15.7-19.4m Continue south and head to Ross Ridge. Go down into a deep canyon wash. There are ropes to assist you in getting down–as pictured. Be careful.

19.4-25.6m Travel west out of the canyon and climb a few ups and downs to the next DT road.

25.6-26.6m Go down the DT south to the next junction.

26.6-28.6m Turn right/W back onto a ST and then veer left (W) at the old corral. Head back to the parking area.

Mileage Estimate

0.0-1.3m Leave the parking lot to the east and cross the road to the ST. Turn left (N) at the dry pond. Prime Cut begins here. Continue to the dirt road.

1.3-2.2m Look across the dirt road to the trail and go north. Continue on this twisting path through the trees to Chutes & Ladder's.

2.2-3.2m Turn left (NW) to the DT road and cross 18 Road to Frontside junction. Then go right (N) past Joe's Ridge.

3.2-3.9m Careful through this section, the trail is on an exposed edge. Veer right (NW) at Zippety Doo Daa along the tight ridge.

3.9-5.0m Go down the steep, rocky switchbacks to the dry wash. Climb out to Western Zip/Zippety Doo Daa at the top.

5.0-11.4m Continue north on Frontside and down a steep hill toward Coal Gulch Road. Go right (E) on Coal Gulch and follow the road past Garvey Canyon Overlook and uphill to the split.

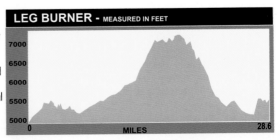

LEG BURNER - MEASURED IN FEET

7000
6500
6000
5500
5000

0   MILES   28.6

Distance: 10.1 miles one way/ 20.2 miles out and back
Elevation Gain: 2,500 feet/1,400 feet   **Use:** Moderate-Heavy
Foot Difficulty: Easy-Difficult   **Biking Difficulty:** Easy-Difficult

Trail Location: From downtown Fruita at the roundabout (Circle Park) go east on Aspen Street. Go 4 blocks to Maple Street, also known as 17 1/2 Road. Turn left (N) and drive 4 miles. Turn right (E) onto N 3/10 Road and follow this to the T intersection at 18 Road. Then turn left (N) on 18 Road and go 4.3 miles to the main parking area. Frontside begins 2 miles up 18 Road from the main parking area. You can also drive this 2 mile section along 18 Road and park on the right (E) side of the road near the trailhead.

North

Mileage Estimate

0.0-2.0m Head north on 18 Road to the upper parking area.

2.0-2.4m Make a left/W at the fence. Go right (N) on the ST to Joe's Ridge junction.

2.4-2.9m At this junction, stay straight(N) .

2.9-3.6m Be careful through this section; the trail is on an exposed edge on the side of a steep hill. Veer right (NW) at the Zippety Doo Daa Trail junction and then travel along the tight ridge.

3.6-4.7m Drop down the steep, rocky switchbacks to the dry wash. Climb out of the wash and to the Western Zip/Zippety Doo Daa Trail junction at the top.

4.7-7.8m Continue north on Frontside and drop down a steep hill toward Coal Gulch Road. Take a right (NE) on Coal Gulch and follow the road past an old mine. The trail continues on the right (S) but is really hard to find. Look for the cairn at this point.

7.8-10.1m Turn right (SE) and climb up a steep, rocky DT that seems to never end. This trail stops along the very top of the Book Cliffs overlooking 18 Road.

10.1-20.2 Turn around and return to the 18 Road parking lot.

Trail Description: Frontside has it all: from easy dirt roads to technical rocky sections on loose hillsides to hazardous steep edges. Frontside will test your endurance and stamina if you do the complete out and back. Western Zip, Zippety Doo Daa, and Joe's Ridge are a few trails that can be tackled in addition, for longer loops.

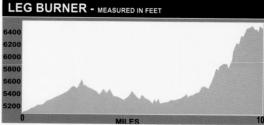

LEG BURNER - MEASURED IN FEET

Distance: 2.7 miles one way/ 5.4 miles out and back
Elevation Gain: 525 feet   **Use:** Moderate-Heavy
Foot Difficulty: Easy-Moderate   **Biking Difficulty:** Moderate

Trail Location: access 1 From downtown Fruita, at the roundabout (Circle Park), go east on Aspen Street. Go 4 blocks to Maple Street, also known as 17 1/2 Road. Turn left (N) and drive 4 miles. Turn right (E) onto N 3/10 Road and follow this to the T intersection at 18 Road. Then turn left (N) on 18 Road and go 4.3 miles to the main parking area. The lower portion of Joe's Ridge starts to the north about 1 mile up 18 Road.
access 2 The upper portion of Joe's Ridge can be accessed by traveling along Frontside to the half mile mark.

North

Mileage Estimate
(starting from access 1)

0.0-0.8m Go left (N) from the parking area to a ST and head northwest.

0.8-1.4m Continue on the ST to the dirt road. Follow the dirt road a short distance to the first right (N) onto a DT.

1.4-2.7m Follow the DT north to the rocky area with the steep ups and downs.

2.7-5.4m At the Frontside Trail junction, turn around and head back or continue to Frontside, Prime Cut and Chutes and Ladders.

Trail Description: Joe's Ridge is a winding ST that is more adventurous than Prime Cut, but is definitely less adventurous than longer trails like Edge Loop. There is a wide spread view of the Grand Valley from the ridge. This is an ideal spot to take a break and a couple of photos. This trail can be mixed and matched with other nearby trails for some even longer adventures.

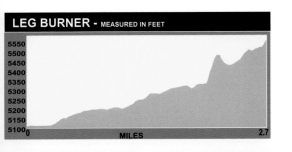

LEG BURNER - MEASURED IN FEET

The Perimeter- Book Cliffs/18 Road

Distance: 12.3 mile loop
Elevation Gain: 1,750 feet
Foot Difficulty: Moderate

Use: Moderate
Biking Difficulty: Moderate-Difficult

Trail Location: From downtown Fruita, at the roundabout (Circle Park), go east on Aspen Street. Go 4 blocks to Maple Street, also known as 17 1/2 Road. Turn left (N) and drive 4 miles. Turn right (E) onto N 3/10 Road and follow this to the T intersection at 18 Road. Then turn left (N) on 18 Road and go 4.3 miles to the main parking area.

Mileage Estimate

0.0-0.7m Go west out of the parking lot on the ST to Zippety Doo Daa .

0.7-1.3m Turn left (S) onto Western Zip and continue to the next junction.

1.3-2.9m Turn right (NW) past the hills onto the rocky dirt road to the next junction.

2.9-3.5m Turn right (N) onto the ST and uphill to the gate.

3.5-4.7m Cross the dirt road to the Frontside Trail junction.

4.7-5.4m Turn right (SE) onto Frontside.

5.4-5.6m Work your way through the wash, up and over the steep switchback.

5.6-6.3m Veer left (E), continuing on Frontside.

6.3-7.0m Go in and out of the dry washes and continue straight (S) past Joe's Ridge Trail junction.

7.0-7.5m Make a left (E) on the dirt road that changes into DT on the way to Chutes & Ladders/Prime Cut Trail junction.

7.5-8.2m Turn left (NE) onto Chutes & Ladders, and go through the steep ups and downs.

8.2-10.3m Cross the dirt road on to the prairie and head to the corral.

10.3-12.3 Turn right (W) on the ST along the fence and back to the dry pond and trail junction. Continue west uphill to the parking area.

Trail Description: The Perimeter is a challenging loop with all 18 Road trails wrapped up into one. It has everything from steep ups and flat prairies to smooth ST and rocky DT. Along this trail, there are some incredible views of the Book Cliffs, the Grand Valley, the Uncompahgre Plateau and all the way to the La Sal Mountains in central Utah.

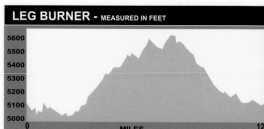

LEG BURNER - MEASURED IN FEET

5600	
5500	
5400	
5300	
5200	
5100	
5000	
0	MILES	12

Distance: 2.2miles one way/ 4.4 miles out and back
Elevation Gain: 525 feet   **Use:** Moderate-Heavy
Foot Difficulty: Easy   **Biking Difficulty:** Easy-Moderate

Trail Location: From downtown Fruita at the roundabout (Circle Park) go east on Aspen Street. Go 4 blocks to Maple Street, also known as 17 1/2 Road. Turn left (N) and drive 4 miles. Turn right (E) onto N 3/10 Road and follow this to the T intersection at 18 Road. Then turn left (N) on 18 Road and go 4.3 miles to the main parking area.

North

Mileage Estimate

0.0-0.2m Leave the parking lot to the east and cross the road to where the ST starts. Go down the hill to the dry pond.

0.2-1.3m Turn left (N) at the dry pond. Prime Cut begins here. Continue to the dirt road.

1.3-2.2m Look straight across the dirt road to the trail and follow the trail that goes north. Continue on this twisting and turning path through the trees to the Chutes and Ladders Trail junction.

2.2-4.4m Return the way you came or try Chutes and Ladders, Frontside, Joe's Ridge or Zippety Doo Daa.

Trail Description: Prime Cut makes a pleasant start to any outing. This narrow and not too difficult path climbs through the juniper trees and approaches the base of the Book Cliffs. The trail may be a little bumpy because of the cattle track ruts crisscrossing the area. Near the top of the trail, the Colorado National Monument is visible.

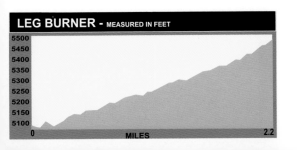

LEG BURNER - MEASURED IN FEET

5500
5450
5400
5350
5300
5250
5200
5150
5100

0   MILES   2.2

Western Zip - Book Cliffs/18 Road

Distance: 4.7 miles one way/ 9.4 miles out and back
Elevation Gain: 750 feet   **Use:** Moderate-Heavy
Foot Difficulty: Easy-Moderate   **Biking Difficulty:** Easy-Moderate

Trail Location: From downtown Fruita, at the roundabout (Circle Park), go east on Aspen Street. Go 4 blocks to Maple Street, also known as 17 1/2 Road. Turn left (N) and drive 4 miles. Turn right (E) onto N 3/10 Road and follow this to the T intersection at 18 Road. Then turn left (N) on 18 Road and go 4.3 miles to the main parking area. Western Zip is accessed at the lower west side of the parking area.

North

Mileage Estimate

0.0-0.7m   Go west out of the parking lot on the ST to the Zippety Doo Daa junction.

0.7-1.3m   Turn left (S) onto Western Zip and continue to the next junction.

1.3-2.9m   Turn right (NW) past the hills onto the rocky dirt road to the next junction.

2.9-3.5m   Turn right (N) onto the ST and uphill to the gate.

3.5-4.7m   Continue on and cross the dirt road to the Frontside junction.

4.7-9.4m   Turn around and head back or extend the fun on Frontside or Zippety Doo Daa.

Trail Description: Along the trail, Western Zip has signs labeling it as Zippety Doo Daa, but it is a separate trail, so it is referred to separately. It goes west of the ridge along the prairie and then north, resulting in a much tamer and less challenging trail than Zippety Doo Daa.

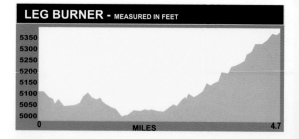

LEG BURNER - MEASURED IN FEET

Zippety Doo Daa - Book Cliffs/18 Road

Distance: 3 miles one way/ 6 miles out and back
Elevation Gain: 700 feet
Foot Difficulty: Easy-Difficult
Use: Moderate-Heavy
Biking Difficulty: Moderate-Difficult

Trail Location: From downtown Fruita, at the roundabout (Circle Park), go east on Aspen Street. Go 4 blocks to Maple Street, also known as 17 1/2 Road. Turn left (N) and drive 4 miles. Turn right (E) onto N 3/10 Road and follow this to the T intersection at 18 Road. Then turn left (N) on 18 Road and go 4.3 miles to the main parking area. Zippety Doo Daa begins on the ST at the lower western side of the parking lot.

Mileage Estimate

0.0-0.7m Follow the ST down and then back up to the DT.

0.7-2.0m Turn right (N) and follow the trail to where the steep ups and downs begin. Continue through the gate and across a dirt road.

2.0-3.0m Cross the dirt road and the fun resumes. You will now understand your urge to sing the song that shares its name with the trail.

3.0-6.0m Head back or continue humming that tune on Frontside, Joe's Ridge or Western Zip.

Trail Description: The name of this trail might make "Zippety Doo Daa, Zippety A, My Oh My, What a Wonderful Day!" go through your head over and over. Although the song gives most people a happy feeling, the trail may not. Don't be discouraged or shy away, the trail can be easy as well as difficult. There are several steep ups and downs and very narrow sections. Those who have a fear of heights might want to think twice before trying this trail.

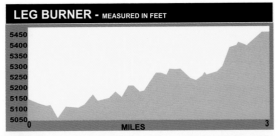

LEG BURNER - MEASURED IN FEET

MILES

116

Hunter's Canyon - Book Cliffs/21 Road

Distance: 6 miles one way/ 12 miles out and back
Elevation Gain: 1,800 feet   **Use:** Moderate
Foot Difficulty: Easy-Moderate   **Biking Difficulty:** Moderate-Difficult

Trail Location: From Grand Junction, take Hwy 6 & 50 northwest for 5 miles turn right (N) on to 21 Road. Follow 21 Road and veer right where the pavement ends. Continue on the dirt road and turn right (N) east at the fork in the road. Follow this road and park when the road becomes impassable. Hunter's Canyon begins 13 miles from the turn off of Highway 6 &50.

North

Mileage Estimate

0.0-4.0m The trail travels within the canyon offering enjoyable views and interesting plant life in some alcoves.

4.0-6.0m Continue up this steep, bumpy road when you reach the natural gas pad where the road is well maintained. The trail levels off just enough to be able to get to the top at 7,000 feet and the Edge Loop junction.

6.0-12.0m Turn around here, fly down the steep road and back through the canyon to the parking area.

Trail Description: Hunter's Canyon begins on an old road that is not maintained, then goes through a very narrow and spooky canyon. Despite this, there are some enjoyable and lush alcoves. At the end, where it meets up with Edge Loop and offers a stunning 360 degree view of the Horse Mountains and the Grand Valley. At this point, you can continue on Edge Loop in either direction. See 18 Road map on page 105.

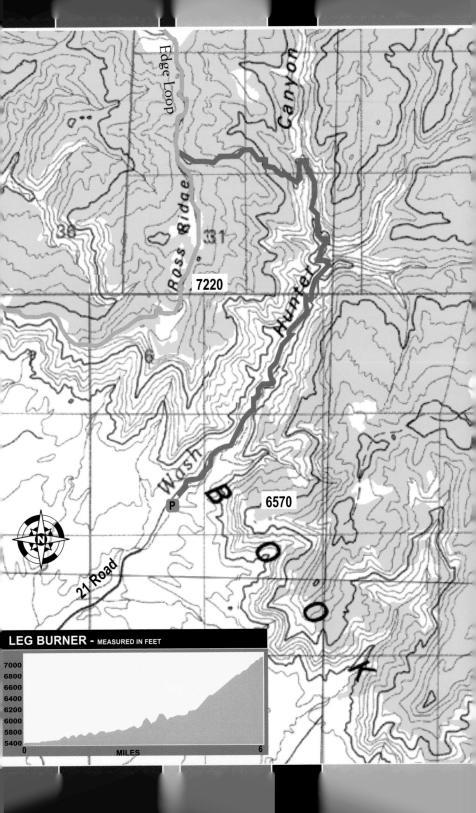

Edge Loop

Canyon

Ross Ridge

Hunter

31

.7220

Wash

P

6570

B O O K

21 Road

LEG BURNER - MEASURED IN FEET

| 7000 |
| 6800 |
| 6600 |
| 6400 |
| 6200 |
| 6000 |
| 5800 |
| 5600 |
| 5400 |

0   MILES   6

N

The Desert - Book Cliffs shown in ▬▬▬▬▬

Distance: .Virtually unlimited miles.
Foot Difficulty: Easy-Moderate

Use: Moderate
Biking Difficulty: Easy-Difficult

Trail Location: Located just north of Grand Junction. Drive 0.9 miles north on 29 Road from Patterson. Park just after crossing the irrigation ditch on the left (N) side of the road.

Mileage Estimate

0.0-0.75m Travel out of the parking area to the northwest on the dirt road to the tunnel. Go through the tunnel and out the wash. All other mileage is up to you.

Trail Description: The Desert makes its way along a sandy, non-technical ST and DT through the hot dry desert, just like the name implies. The trail makes its way northeast along Walker Field Airport property and then directly into the Book Cliffs. The path is loose and rocky, especially through the tunnel, and is covered with thorns, so it is wise to bring extra tubes for your tires. Take any of the surrounding dirt adobe trails toward the Book Cliffs in any direction. Just go out and have fun exploring, but beware of the heavy ATV and other motorized traffic in this area on the weekends.

North

Roller Coaster - Book Cliffs/The Desert shown in ▬▬▬▬▬

Distance: Virtually unlimited miles
Foot Difficulty: Easy-Moderate

Use: Heavy
Biking Difficulty: Easy-Moderate

Trail Location: access 1 From Horizon Drive and I-70, go north on Horizon toward the airport. Turn left (NW) on H Road, in front of the large jet. Follow H Road and turn right (NE) onto 27 Road. Drive north just over 1 mile. Park here on the right (E) hand side of the road in a huge parking area.

Trail Description: The Roller Coaster area has many choices for varying trails. Head out to the tall, steep adobe hills and pick a trail. It is very difficult to follow the same way back, so simply head back in the same direction in which you came or turn in a southwesterly direction. If you come upon the airport fence line, follow it west to the parking area. This area has a lot of ATV and motorized vehicle traffic, especially on the weekends.

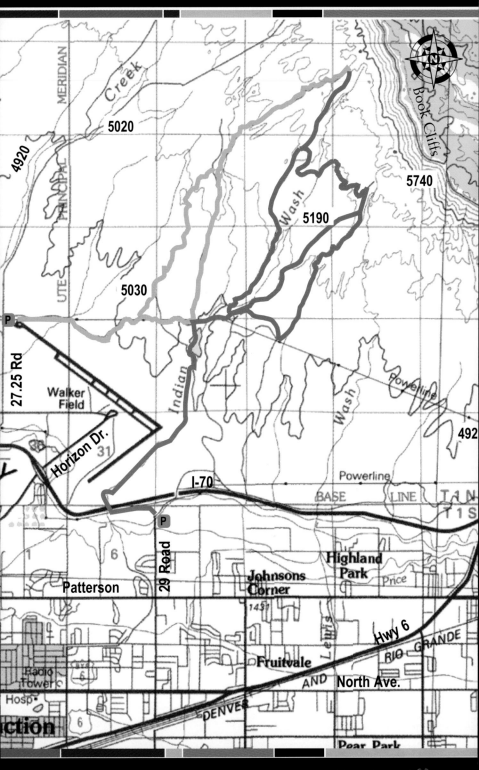

N
Book Cliffs

MERIDIAN
Creek
5020
4920
PRINCIPAL
UTE
5740
Wash
5190
5030

P
27.25 Rd
Walker
Field
Indian
Horizon Dr.
31
Wash
Powerline
492

I-70
Powerline
BASE LINE T 1 N
T 1 S
P
6
29 Road
Highland Park
Johnsons Corner
Price
Patterson
1451
Radio Tower
6
Fruitvale
Hwy 6
RIO GRANDE
AND
North Ave.
Hosp
6
DENVER
:tion
Pear Park

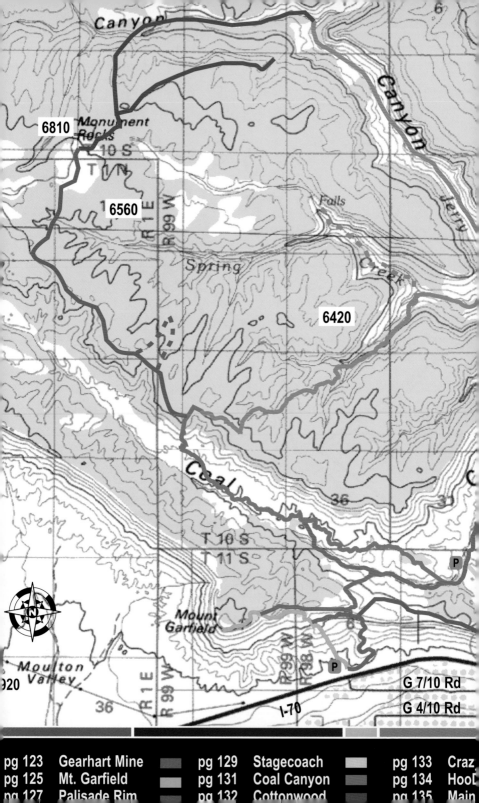

6810

Monument
Rocks

T 10 S

T 11 N

6560

R 1 E

R 99 W

Canyon

Canyon

Jerry

Falls

Spring

Creek

6420

Coal

36

T 10 S

T 11 S

Mount
Garfield

P

Moulton
Valley

920

36

R 1 E

R 99 W

R 98 W

P

I-70

N

G 7/10 Rd

G 4/10 Rd

5740

Asbur...

Creek

Whittaker

Flats

Creek

Tunnel
No. 1

ISLAND A
STATE RE

P 1796

P

exit 46

Coal Gulch

Cameo

Tunnel
No. 2

I-70

Mount
Lincoln

6650

1985

Baile
Point

Tunnel
No. 3

Go Boy
Mine

Palisade
Mines

5740

P

Midwest
Mine

Palisade

Gearhart Mine - Book Cliffs/Mt Garfield

Distance: 2.5 miles one way/ 5 miles out and back
Elevation Gain: 2,250 feet   **Use:** Moderate
Foot Difficulty: Moderate-Difficult

Trail Location: From Grand Junction, take I-70 east toward Palisade. Exit at #42 and turn right (S) . Make another right (W) onto G 3/10 Road. Follow this road for around 1.5 miles and turn right (N) and under I-70. Park on the north side of the interstate. Gearhart Mine starts outside of the fenced area to the east. See the Book Cliff/Mt. Garfield map on page 121.

Mileage Estimate

0.0-1.0m Go east out of the parking area and along I-70. The trail turns north and starts up the Book Cliffs.

1.0-1.5m At the first ridge, turn left (W) to the 4x4 road. Stay right (N) and then make your way to the left (W) around the rock wall. This trail joins Coal Canyon which comes from the canyon below.

1.5-2.0m Continue west on this rocky DT to where the road ends at an overlook. Continue on the faint trail to the right (NW), down into a small canyon and back out. Go down into a dry wash, veering left (W) to the base of the ridge just below Mt. Garfield.

2.0-2.5m The last half mile is a steep climb up around 400 feet to where it levels off on the way to the flagpole with an awesome overlook and views of the valley.

2.5-3.0m Turn around and go back to the ridge just below Mt. Garfield.

3.0-3.5m Stay straight and follow the Mt. Garfield trail along the exposed section to the Gearhart Mine junction.

3.5-4.0m Turn left (E) just before the main trail drops off a lower ridge to the south. Go across the ridgeline and past the Gearhart mine and back onto the trail you came in on.

4.0-5.0m Make a right (S) here and back down the steep, rocky, loose trail back to the parking area.

Trail Description: Gearhart Mine is just as difficult as Mt. Garfield, but is longer by 1 mile. In some places, the trail is hard to find so make sure you have a map and a compass. This trail also has stunning views of the farmland around Palisade and requires some agility to climb up and around the boulders on the very steep mountain.

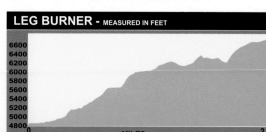

LEG BURNER - MEASURED IN FEET

6600
6400
6200
6000
5800
5600
5400
5200
5000
4800
0   2.
MILES

Garfield's
OFF BROADWAY

Baked
Broiled
Blackened
Flat Grilled
Deep Fried
Garlic & Olive Oil
Dijon
Cajun Style

Garfield's offers the largest selection of fresh fish and sumptuous seafood in the Grand Valley, accompanied by fine wine & spirits. Our award winning chef and knowledgeable staff will assure a memorable dining experience. Enjoy breathtaking views of the Monument and watch the fiery Colorado sunset as you dine on our enclosed patio.

Located at 2148 Broadway, In the Redlands, Grand Junction, Colorado 970.245.8080
Cocktail Lounge and Dinning Room are open Monday thru Saturday 4 to 10 p.m.

Distance: 2 miles out and back
Elevation Gain: 2,000 feet   **Use:** Moderate
Foot Difficulty: Difficult-Insane

Trail Location: From Grand Junction, take I-70 east toward Palisade. Take exit #42 and turn right (S) . Make another right (W) onto G 3/10 Road. Follow this road for around 1.5 miles and turn right (N) and under I-70. Park on the north side of the interstate.

North

Mileage Estimate

0.0-0.5m   Begin from the map board to the steep uphill ascent and along a very exposed ridge for approximately 600 feet elevation climb.

0.5-1.0m   Here the uphill climb continues in and around boulders up the mountainside to a plateau.

1.0-1.5m   Pass the Lower Gearhart Mine junction. Continue with a more moderate climb to the base of a mountain wall along an exposed edge to the ridge just below Mt. Garfield.

1.5-2.0m   The last half mile is a steep climb up 400 feet to where it levels off on the way to the flagpole and an awesome overlook.

2.0-4.0m   Turn around and head back the way you came.

Trail Description: Mt. Garfield could be considered the most strenuous 2 mile trail up any mountain in the region. This trail is not recommended for casual hikers or young children. Being surefooted is mandatory on the uphills and downhills because of the steep ascents and descents on this trail. There are spectacular views of everything in every direction.

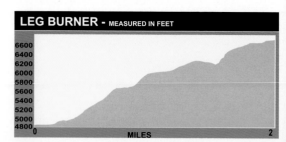

LEG BURNER - MEASURED IN FEET

6600	
6400	
6200	
6000	
5800	
5600	
5400	
5200	
5000	
4800	
0	MILES 2

Palisade Rim- Book Cliffs/Mt Garfield

Distance: 3 miles one way/ 6 miles out and back
Elevation Gain: 600 feet   **Use:** Moderate
Foot Difficulty: Moderate

Trail Location: This trail is located just off I-70, but not at any exit. From Grand Junction, take I-70 east to Cameo Exit #46. Turn left (NW) under the overpass and back out on to I-70 and heading west. You will now be traveling back to Grand Junction. Follow I-70 west for 1.5 miles and look right (N) just after you cross the bridge over the Colorado River. Make a quick right (N) turn and park just off the interstate at the parking area. The Palisade Rim trail begins off the Stagecoach Trail at 1.7 miles.

North

Mileage Estimate

0.0-0.9m The trail is rocky and narrow along the rim as it goes into a rocky wash. There is no formal trail to the flagpole, so be careful.

0.9-1.8m Now there is a faint trail that travels west across the rim at the top of the Book Cliffs. The trail runs into a large area of slickrock which needs to be climbed to be able to continue the trail across the rim.

1.8-3.0m Past the slickrock, you arrive at the section that will put the fear of God in you. It is a narrow path that slants downward, balancing right on the edge, and is covered in loose, broken shale. After that section, the trail continues along the edge and meets up with the Coal Canyon road which goes up the back of the Book Cliffs.

3.0-6.0m Turn around and head back. There are a couple of different routes that can be taken to get to the beginning of this trail, so if you have the exploration time, take one of them.

Trail Description: Palisade Rim makes its way up along the rim of the Book Cliffs and portions of the slickrock. There are a few scary and very dangerous areas along the trail, so take these into consideration when planning to hike this trail. If you are in good shape and have some basic climbing skills to attempt the entire trail, your reward will be some breathtaking views of the Grand Valley. Also note that this trail crosses private property so please be courteous.

LEG BURNER - MEASURED IN FEET

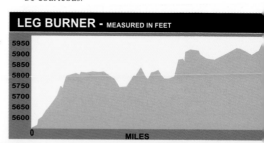

127

Stagecoach-Book Cliffs/Mt. Garfield

Distance: 3.8 miles one way/7.6 miles out and back
Elevation Gain: 1,300 feet/800 feet   **Use:** Moderate
Foot Difficulty: Moderate   **Biking Difficulty:** Moderate-Difficult

Trail Location: This trail is located just off I-70, but not at any exit. From Grand Junction, take I-70 east to the Cameo Exit #46. Turn left (NW) under the overpass and back out on to I-70. You will now be heading back to Grand Junction. Follow I-70 back toward Grand Junction for 1.5 miles and look right (N) just after you cross the bridge. Make a quick right (N) turn and park off the interstate at the parking area. You can also park at the Grande River Vineyards. They offer free day passes for hikers and bikers if you check in at the front desk, and start the trail by going under the I-70 overpass.

North

Mileage Estimate

0.0-0.5m   This trail begins with a climb up a steep rocky section along and above I-70 & the Colorado River.

0.5-1.7m   Here the trail levels off and gently climbs below to the south of Mt. Lincoln as it makes its way to an overlook. Then it goes back into a wash and to the Palisade Rim junction.

1.7-2.6m   Veer right (NW) and continue to climb up toward the southwestern edge of Mt. Lincoln and along a small canyon wash. Continue on to the next trail junction.

2.6-3.8m   Turn right (NW) onto the unmarked ST and downhill through a couple of gates to the 4x4 road which drops downhill to the base of Coal Canyon.

3.8-7.6m   Head back or continue on Coal Canyon.

Trail Description: Stagecoach is a fun trail that makes its way up the beginning edge of the Book Cliffs next to the Grand Mesa. It offers dazzling views of the Grand Valley, Mount Lincoln and the Palisade vineyards. There is an old surface coal mining site along the back side. This trail crosses private property so please respect the land.

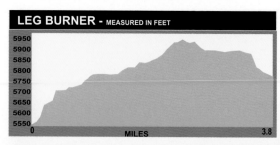

LEG BURNER - MEASURED IN FEET

5950
5900
5850
5800
5750
5700
5650
5600
5550

0   MILES   3.8

Coal Canyon - Wild Horse Range/Little Book Cliffs WSA

Distance: 5 miles one way/ 10 miles out and back
Elevation Gain: 1,750 feet   **Use:** Moderate-Heavy
Foot Difficulty: Easy-Moderate   **Biking Difficulty:** Easy-Difficult

Trail Location: From Grand Junction, take I-70 east to the Cameo Exit #46. Turn left (NW) and go under I-70. Pass the on and off ramp to I-70 and follow the road to the right (NE) toward the power plant. Turn left (N) and drive over the Colorado River. Pass by the power plant over the small bridge and veer right (NE) at the public access road. Follow this narrow unmaintained road for around 1.5 miles, and stay straight to the parking area and the gated fence.

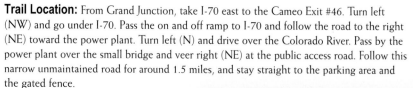

North

Mileage Estimate

0.0-2.9m   Pass through the gate along the DT and continue in and alongside the canyon wash.

2.9-3.5m   Veer left (W) and down the hill, continuing into the canyon. A right (N) will take you to the HooDoo. junction

3.5-3.8m   Stay in the base of the canyon, and look to the left (SW) for the next trail junction.

3.8-5.0m   Turn left (SW) up the DT and climb the switchbacks through the trees on the way to the Mt. Garfield viewing area. The trail ends here at the edge.

5.0-10.0m   Turn around or continue down Gearhart Mine.

Trail Description: Coal Canyon got its name from the surface coal mines that used to mine the area. The trail is a gentle, moderate climb with some difficult switchbacks near the end. It can also be soggy in the canyon during the wet season. Hikers can continue in the canyon wash at the 3.5 to 3.8 mile section to extend the outing. At the end of this wash, you will have to turn around and head back and make the left (SW) turn. It is not recommended for mountain bikers to extend their trip in this manner, as the wash becomes too sandy and soft. Join up with Stagecoach to make a great loop.

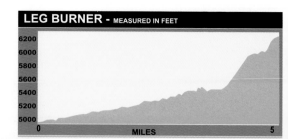

LEG BURNER - MEASURED IN FEET

131

Cottonwood Trail - Wild Horse Range/Little Book Cliffs WSA

Distance: 3.5 miles one way/ 7 miles out and back
Elevation Gain: 1,500 feet   **Use:** Light
Foot Difficulty: Moderate

Trail Location: From Grand Junction, take I-70 east to the Cameo Exit #46. Turn left (W) and go under I-70. Pass the on and off ramp to I-70 and follow the road to the right (N) toward the power plant. Turn left (W) and drive over the Colorado River. Pass by the power plant over the small bridge and veer right (N) at the public access road. Follow this narrow unmaintained road for around 1.5 miles, and stay straight to the parking area and the gated fence. Cottonwood begins 5.2 miles along Main Canyon.

North

Mileage Estimate

0.0-2.0m Turn left (W) away from Main Canyon and follow along the left (S) side of Cottonwood Canyon to begin climbing.

2.0-3.0m Climb away from Cottonwood Canyon and creek to the next trail junction.

3.0-3.5m Turn right (W) to the end of the trail and Monument Rocks.

3.5-7.0m Head back or continue on Crazy Ed.

Trail Description: Cottonwood is through the Wild Horse Range/Little Book Cliffs near Main Canyon. At the 3.0 mile trail junction, there is a path off to the east that travels downhill to Cottonwood Spring. Keep in mind that you will have to climb back out to the trail. Wild horses can be seen in the area, Horse Mountain can be viewed to the north along with the Monument Rock formations at the end of the trail.

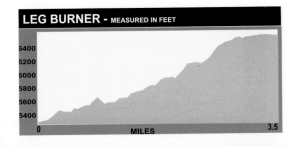

LEG BURNER - MEASURED IN FEET

6400
6200
6000
5800
5600
5400

0   MILES   3.5

Crazy Ed - Wild Horse Range/Little Book Cliffs WSA

Distance: 3.6 miles one way/ 7.2 miles out and back
Elevation Gain: 450 feet/ 450 feet   **Use:** Light
Foot Difficulty: Easy-Moderate

Trail Location: From Grand Junction, take I-70 east to the Cameo Exit #46. Turn left (NW) and go under I-70. Pass the on and off ramp to I-70 and follow the road to the right (N) toward the power plant. Turn left (NW) and drive over the Colorado River. Pass by the power plant over the small bridge and veer right (NE) at the public access road. Follow this narrow unmaintained road for around 1.5 miles, and stay straight to the parking area and the gated fence. The fence is open for vehicle travel from June 1st through November 30. During this time period, you can drive along the road for another 2.8 miles and make a right (SW) turn and park at the flat natural gas pad area and the trailhead. Crazy Ed begins 4.8 miles along HooDoo.

Mileage Estimate

0.0-0.7m Go north away from HooDoo to the trail junction on your right (NE) . This path leads to Adobe Springs.

0.7-2.8m Continue along the ridge to the northwest where the trail becomes a DT road for a short distance to the next trail junction.

2.8-3.6m The trail turns right (NE) away from the road and travels just along the northern edge of Spring Creek Canyon to the Crazy Ed Spring and the end of the trail.

3.6-7.2m Head back or continue on Cottonwood.

Trail Description: Crazy Ed follows along HooDoo and along the rim through the junipers and past several springs to a rock formation known as Monument Rock. Wild horses can be seen along the way and a short side trip can be made to Adobe Springs. Continue on past Adobe Springs and back out to Crazy Ed.

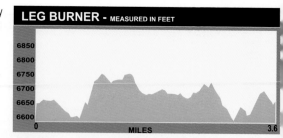

LEG BURNER - MEASURED IN FEET

6850
6800
6750
6700
6650
6600

0   MILES   3.6

HooDoo Trail - Wild Horse Range/Little Book Cliffs WSA

Distance: 4.8 miles one way/ 9.6 miles out and back
Elevation Gain: 1,740 feet **Use:** Moderate
Foot Difficulty: Moderate-Difficult

Trail Location: From Grand Junction, take I-70 east to the Cameo Exit #46. Turn left (NW) and go under I-70. Pass the on and off ramp to I-70 and follow the road to the right (E) toward the power plant. Turn left (NW) and drive over the Colorado River. Pass by the power plant over the small bridge and veer right (NE) at the public access road. Follow this narrow unmaintained road for around 1.5 miles, and stay straight to the parking area and the gated fence. The fence is open for vehicle travel from June 1st through November 30. During this time period, you can drive along the road for another 2.8 miles and make a right (N) turn and park at the flat natural gas pad area and the trailhead.

North

Mileage Estimate

0.0-2.7m Begin this trail from the natural gas pad and roller coaster up and down the DT following the trail markers.

2.7-3.8m As the trail makes its way into a small canyon wash, it turns into an ST. Follow this ST along the right side of Coal Canyon as you approach three large HooDoo rock structures pictured on this page. Just past these structures, there is a steep climb.

3.8-4.8m Around 100 yards or so past the three HooDoos, look to the right (N) for the cairn marker. Turn right (N) and climb, climb, climb. The trail can be hard to follow at this point, as it switches back and forth through the narrow, sandy, and rocky section to the top.

4.8-9.6m Head back down or continue on Crazy Ed or Spring Canyon.

Trail Description: Hoo Doo is half DT and half ST, making its way above the Coal Canyon wash and along the back of the Book Cliffs. The final portion of this trail is a severe climb uphill. There are some amazing views of the back of the Book Cliffs and Mt. Garfield with several trails snaking their way up the back of Mt. Garfield.

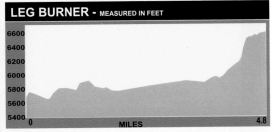

LEG BURNER - MEASURED IN FEET

Main Canyon- Wild Horse Range/Little Book Cliffs WSA

Distance: 5.2 miles one way/ 10.4 out and back
Elevation Gain: 825 feet/ 500 feet   **Use:** Light
Foot Difficulty: Easy-Moderate

Trail Location: From Grand Junction, take I-70 east to the Cameo Exit #46. Turn left (NW) and go under I-70. Pass the on and off ramp to I-70 and follow the road to the right (E) toward the power plant. Turn left (NW) and drive over the Colorado River. Pass by the power plant over the small bridge and veer right (NE) at the public access road. Follow this narrow unmaintained road for around 1.5 miles, and stay straight to the parking area and the gated fence.

North

Mileage Estimate

0.0-1.3m Take the ST on the right (NE) as you pass through the gate. Then go up and over the small ridge to the overlook of Main Canyon. Drop down the steep ST into the base of the canyon next to Jerry Creek and into the Wild Horse Range/Little Book Cliffs WSA. The trail becomes DT, moving in and out of the creek up to the Spring Creek Junction.

1.3-5.2m Turn right (NW) and continue winding in and out to the Round Mountain and Cottonwood junctions.

5.2-10.4m Turn around and head back to the parking area or continue on Round Mountain or Cottonwood.

Trail Description: Main Canyon climbs up a gradual canyon with some unusual views of rock structures and arches that are just forming. It can be extremely hot during the summer months, at which time there is usually water filling Jerry's Creek. It provides a perfect opportunity to see many of the wild horses that call this area home.

LEG BURNER - MEASURED IN FEET

5300	
5250	
5200	
5150	
5100	
5050	
5000	
4950	

0   MILES   5

Spring Creek Canyon - Wild Horse Range/Little Book Cliffs WSA

Distance: 5 miles one way/ 10 miles out and back
Elevation Gain: 1,850 feet   **Use:** Light
Foot Difficulty: Moderate-Difficult

Trail Location: From Grand Junction, take I-70 east to the Cameo Exit #46. Turn left (NW) and go under I-70. Pass the on and off ramp to I-70 and follow the road to the right (E) toward the power plant. Turn left (NW) and drive over the Colorado River. Pass by the power plant over the small bridge and veer right (NE) at the public access road. Follow this narrow unmaintained road for around 1.5 miles, and stay straight to the parking area and the gated fence. Spring Canyon begins 1.3 miles up Main Canyon.

North

LEG BURNER - MEASURED IN FEET

Mileage Estimate

0.0-1.2m Follow the cairns and orange markers as the trail starts in Spring Canyon wash to the left (W) of Main Canyon.

1.2-2.7m Here the canyon splits into two and the trail goes through the wash on the left (W). Inside the wash, look left (S) for an ST trail that climbs up and out of the wash on the left (SW) side of this canyon. The trail joins the base of the canyon just before the canyon splits into two. A right (NW) here goes through the main artery of Spring Creek Canyon to a waterfall.

2.7-5.0m The trail is hard to find where the canyon splits again. Look carefully for the orange markers to travel up and out of the canyon.

5.0-10.0m Go back or continue on HooDoo or Crazy Ed.

Trail Description: Spring Canyon trail begins 1.3 mile along Main Canyon and then travels into turns into the Spring Creek Canyon. There are several bright orange markers nailed to the juniper trees that have arrows pointing in the correct direction to help you find your way. Where there are no trees, cairns mark the trail. There are many wild horses to be seen as you follow the trail to the top of the ridge behind the Book Cliffs.

Tellerico Trail - Book Cliffs/25 Road WSA

Distance: 4.4 miles one way/ 8.8 miles out and back
Elevation Gain: 2,250 feet/1,000 feet   **Use:** Moderate
Foot Difficulty: Moderate-Difficult

Trail Location: Travel north out of Grand Junction from the intersection of Patterson and 25 Road for 10.6 miles. Stay straight at the 6.9 mile mark and park at the open area on the right (E) hand side of the road. Tellerico begins on private property so please be respectful.

North

Mileage Estimate

0.0-0.5m This trail starts on an old 4x4 road into a canyon wash. Follow the wash a short distance and look to the left (N) for the cairns and the trail climbing uphill.

0.5-2.0m From here, the trail roller coasters 1,500 feet up and down as you work your way to Corcoran Point.

2.0-2.4m The trail is not done climbing yet; there are a few 100 or more feet on a soft and loose trail to where the trail splits.

2.4-4.4m Veer left (NW) at the top and travel along the rim as the trail gently descends to the large slickrock area. Then go up and over the ridge to the V. 90 road. If you veer right (E) , follow this trail a short distance to the V.20 Road and then back.

4.4-8.8m Be careful on the way back, for the downhill is steep but feels more loose than going up.

Trail Description: Tellerico is a difficult hiking trail taking you northwest along the face of the Book Cliffs and has beautiful views of Grand Junction and the Uncompahgre Plateau. Many wild horses can be seen as you make your way through the juniper trees.

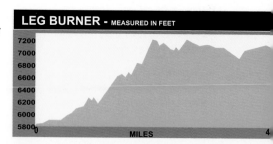

LEG BURNER - MEASURED IN FEET

7200	
7000	
6800	
6600	
6400	
6200	
6000	
5800	

MILES   4

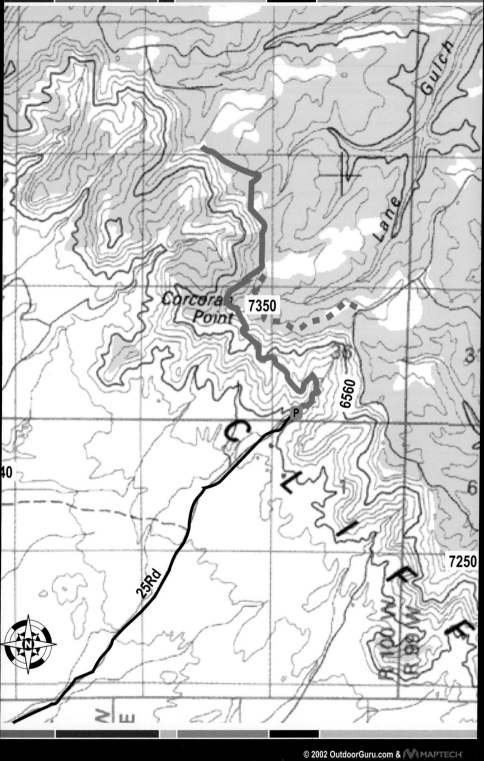

Lane Gulch

Corcoran Point

7350

6560

P

CLIFF

R 100 W
R 99 W

25Rd

40

3

6

7250

N
E

N

OutdoorGuru Thanks
Running Outfitters for
being a sponsor of
the Grand Junction Trails
and Camping Guide.

East

𝒯he Grand Mesa is an exemplary compliment to the Grand Valley's lower elevation. The subalpine forest of Douglas Fir and Engelmann Spruce harbors exceptional trails and forest service road excursions high above the sweltering valley. Summertime temperatures on the Mesa, at over 10,000-feet, are far cooler and a welcome escape from the hot mid-summer days in the Grand Valley. The forested mountainsides with tranquil paths offer distant views and year round activity for all outdoor enthusiasts. With several trails branching from the slopes of Powderhorn to countless alpine lakes, this is a great place to bring the family or dog to enjoy the array of bike trails, hiking trails, fishing holes, camping sites, and cross country ski trails for all ages. Elk herds, porcupines, mule deer and even the rare pine marten can all be seen on the Mesa. Early turning of the exceptional golden aspens occur due to the solitary basalt talus fields, which retain moisture and nighttime cold to encourage exceptional all foliage. An extended stay on the Mesa is easy in the National Forest campgrounds or privately owned resorts and cabins.

Some time or another you will need one.
Make sure you take along some basic items like a few adhesive strips, sterile gauze pads, a roll of athletic tape, extra socks, water purifying tablets, a Mylar blanket, matches and a knife.

The importance of a first-aid kit

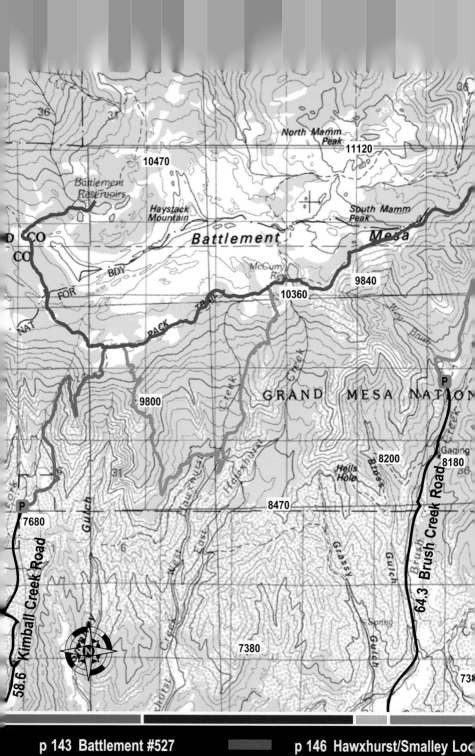

North Mamm Peak

11120

10470

Battlement Reservoirs

Haystack Mountain

South Mamm Peak

D CO

CO

Battlement *Mesa*

BDY

McCum Res

FOR

9840

10360

NAT

PACK

TRAIL

9800

Creek

Creek

GRAND MESA NATION

P

8200

Hells Hole

8180

Gaging

Brush

West Brush

Creek

Hawxhurst

Holuxhurst

P

7680

8470

West

Creek

Kimball Creek Road

Gulch

Grassy

Gulch

Brush Creek Road

64.3

N

7380

Spring Gulch

C

73

58.6

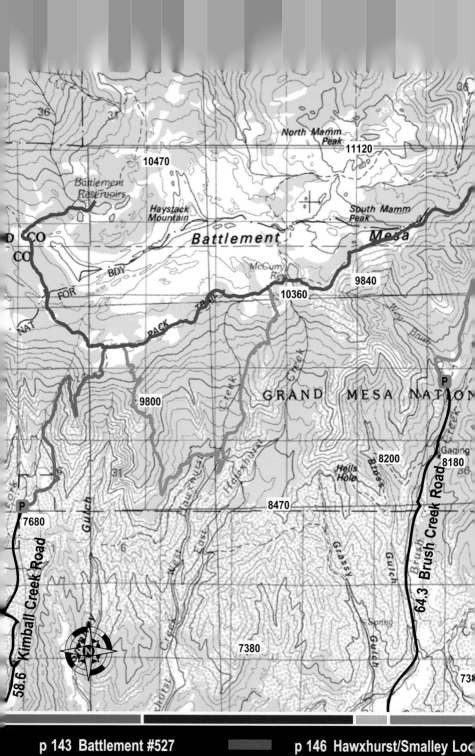

Battlement #527 - Grand Mesa National Forest

Distance: 25.5 miles one way/ 51 miles out and back
Elevation Gain: 5,500 feet/ 11,000   **Use:** Moderate
Foot Difficulty: Moderate   **Biking Difficulty:** Moderate-Difficult

Trail Location: East out of Grand Junction on I-70 to Exit #49. Turn right (S) on State Hwy 65. After 10 miles, turn left/east onto State Hwy 330 for 18 miles through Collbran. Make a left/east at the Y intersection on E330/FR 270. Continue on FR 270 for around 15 miles, and make a left (N) onto FR 271. Follow this road and park at the trailhead 4 miles up the road.

East

Mileage Estimate

0.0-3.0m   This trail parallels Middleton Creek to the lowest elevation of 8,000 feet.

3.0-9.5m   Turn northwest, passing Windy Point to the top of Bald Mountain at an elevation of 10,600 feet.

9.5-12.2m   Continue to East Brush Creek on the left (S) as the trail roller coasters along the north side of the Grand Mesa National Forest.

12.2-13.5m   Stay straight (NW) and clamber up to Brush Creek junction.

13.5-18.2m   Stay straight (W), passing McCurry Reservoir at around 17.5 miles, then on to Hawxhurst and Trail #1903 junction.

Trail Description: Battlement runs through pine trees, meadows and has striking views of Collbran, Rifle, and the Grand Mesa. This trail goes past at least one commercial campsite, so it makes an ideal multiple day backpacking excursion when combined into a loop with Trail #2160 in the White River National Forest

18.2-25.5m   Go past Hawxhurst, Smalley Mountain and Kimball Creek trails located on the left (S). Continue west into the White River National Forest to the commercial campsite(pictured right). Continue another mile and turn right (NE) to the Battlement Reservoirs.

25.5-51.0m   Turn around or take Trail #2160.

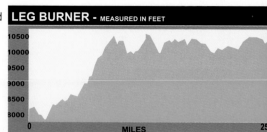

LEG BURNER - MEASURED IN FEET

MILES

143

Brush Creek #529 - Grand Mesa National Forest

Distance: 4 miles one way/ 8 miles out and back
Elevation Gain: 2,050 feet   **Use:** Moderate
Foot Difficulty: Moderate-Difficult   **Biking Difficulty:** Moderate-Difficult

Trail Location: East out of Grand Junction on I-70 to Exit #49. Turn right (S) on State Hwy 65. After 10 miles, turn left/east onto State Hwy 330 for 17.6 miles through Collbran. Make a left (N) onto 64.3/Brush Creek Road. Follow Brush Creek for 2.2 miles and veer left (NW) at the Y intersection. Park at the trailhead 4 miles up the road.

.

East

Mileage Estimate

0.0-1.0m The trail runs next to a property fence to the East Brush Creek junction. The trail sign is broken and is propped up against the fence.

1.0-2.5m Veer left (N) and go through the aspens and a few small creek beds.

2.5-4.0m The trail rises steeply to the end of the trail.

4.0-8.0m Turn around or continue on Battlement.

Trail Description: Brush Creek goes up and along Brush Creek to the northernmost point of the Grand Mesa National Forest. At the top, there are dramatic panoramas and the possibility of a loop with Battlement. This area is covered with little creeks and mosquitoes, so make sure to bring along bug spray.

LEG BURNER - MEASURED IN FEET

10200
10000
9800
9600
9400
9200
9000
8800
8600

0   MILES   4

East Brush Creek #504- Grand Mesa National Forest

Distance: 3 miles one way/ 6 miles out and back
Elevation Gain: 1,650 feet   **Use:** Moderate
Foot Difficulty: Moderate-Difficult   **Biking Difficulty:** Moderate-Difficult

Trail Location: East of Grand Junction on I-70 to Exit #49. Turn right (S) on State Hwy 65. After 10 miles, turn left/east on State Hwy 330 for 17.6 miles through Collbran. Make a left (N) onto 64.3/Brush Creek Road. Follow Brush Creek Road 2.2 miles to a left (NW) at the Y intersection. Park at the trailhead 4 miles ahead. East Brush Creek begins on the right (NE) 1 mile along Brush Creek.

East

Mileage Estimate

0.0-2.0m Turn right (NE) at the trail junction in the open field just north of the property fence. Follow this trail through an aspen grove to the creek crossing below.

2.0-3.0m Head northeast up a moderate climb to the top and the Battlement junction.

3.0-6.0m Turn around or add Battlement or Brush Creek Trail.

Trail Description: East Brush Creek makes its way up the East Fork of Brush Creek through the trees to a small stream. This area can be wet and covered with mosquitoes and ATV traffic. At the top, the trail has marvelous views of the Grand Mesa to the southwest and Rifle to the north.

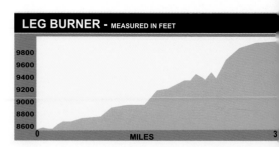

LEG BURNER - MEASURED IN FEET

9800		
9600		
9400		
9200		
9000		
8800		
8600		
0	MILES	3

Hawxhurst #530/Smalley Mountain Loop #531

Distance: 10.1 mile loop
Elevation Gain: 2,900 feet
Foot Difficulty: Moderate-Difficult

Use: Moderate
Biking Difficulty: Difficult

Trail Location: East out of Grand Junction on I-70 to Exit #49. Turn right (S) on State Hwy 65. After 10 miles, turn left/east onto State Hwy 330 for 11.2 miles to Collbran and drive through town and make a left (W) at the T intersection onto 58.6/Kimball Creek Road. Follow Kimball Creek for 6 miles to the Kimball Creek Forest Access sign. Turn right/east and drive a short distance to the Kimball Creek Trailhead parking area. Hawxhurst/Smalley Mountain Loop begins 4.0 miles east along Kimball Creek and then 0.4 miles along Battlement.

East

Mileage Estimate

0.0-2.5m Begin the loop at the Smalley Mountain/Battlement junction, traveling east along the Battlement trail across the glade and open meadows to the Hawxhurst junction.

2.5-5.9m Turn right (S) and down this sometimes steep trail and through the mountain saddle to the Smalley Mountain junction.

5.9-7.5m Turn right (W) and continue straight through the next junction and then west on the trail to the hard right uphill.

7.5-10.1m Go up a ridge at 9,800 feet and then back down toward the Battlement junction and the end of the loop.

Trail Description: The Hawxhurst/Smalley Mountain Loop is physically challenging and is a monster trail in length. A portion of the total 20 miles consists of getting to the start of the loop via Kimball Creek. The old accesses for Hawxhurst and Smalley Mountain at the bottom are now on private property and there is no trespassing. There is camping allowed anywhere in the area, so you can make this loop a part of a multiple day trip and include Battlement.

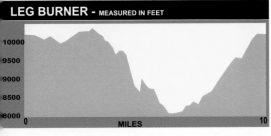

LEG BURNER - MEASURED IN FEET

10000
9500
9000
8500
8000

0   MILES   10

Kimball Creek #532 - Grand Mesa National Forest

Distance: 4.4 miles one way/ 8.8 miles out and back
Elevation Gain: 3,200 feet   **Use:** Moderate
Foot Difficulty: Moderate-Difficult   **Biking Difficulty:** Difficult

Trail Location: East out of Grand Junction on I-70 to Exit #49. Turn right (S) on State Hwy 65. After 10 miles, turn left/east onto State Hwy 330 for 11.2 miles to Collbran and drive through town and make a left (W) at the T intersection onto 58.6/Kimball Creek Road. Follow Kimball Creek for 6 miles to the Kimball Creek Forest Access sign. Turn right/east and drive a short distance to the Kimball Creek Trailhead parking area.

East

Trail Description: Kimball Creek is a steep and narrow ATV trail that is eroded in the center so it is a struggle to follow it and get up the mountain. The mosquitoes can be thick in this area, so bringing along a can of bug spray will provide a bit of comfort. You might break up the trek into more than one day by camping anywhere along the trail.

Mileage Estimate

0.0-2.5m This trail is mostly steep and eroded, which makes it difficult to follow. Sections of ST switchbacks have been added to alleviate this erosion.

2.5-3.0m Now you reach the flat ridge overlooking Collbran.

3.0-4.0m The trail turns back to the north and through a tough and very rocky area and next to the oak brush and alpine grass.

4.0-4.4m The trail tops off and meets up with Battlement.

4.4-8.8m Turn around or go either direction on Battlement.

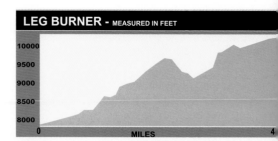

LEG BURNER - MEASURED IN FEET

Powderhorn
Ski Area

36   31   9840   West   M E S A

6   10260

1   A
R

G R A N D

G
R
A
N
D
Creek

on-Jacobs
2

Gill Creek

Deep Creek

Hollenbe
Res No 2

Deep
Res N

P

N

eek   Trail   Creek

Coon Creek
Res No 4

West
Griffith Lake

Water Dog Reservoir

.9160

Hwy 65

NATIONAL

P

Sunset
Lake

P

Skyway

Campgrounds 36

Mesa Lake

Skyway
Point

Su
Rese

South
Mesa Lake

Lost
Lake

erson
No 2

1

No 6

No 8

10650

Anderson Reservoir Rd

on
1

Grand Mesa Reservoirs

Mesa Creek

Lands End Rd

MESA

Flowing Park Rd

Kannah

10360

Res
Clear
Lake

Carson
Lake

A Co

TRAIL

Deep Creek #709/Cutoff #709.1A - Grand Mesa

Distance: 6.5 miles one way/ 13 miles out and back
Elevation Gain: 800 feet/ 1,000 feet **Use:** Moderate
Foot Difficulty: Easy-Difficult
Biking Difficulty: Moderate-Difficult

Trail Location: Around 45 miles from Grand Junction, east on I-70. Take Exit #49 and turn right (S) on State Hwy 65. Go 25 miles to Mesa Lakes Resort. Turn right (SE) and park near the Mesa Lakes restaurant. Deep Creek begins southwest of Sunset Lake at the Glacier Springs Picnic Grounds. Deep Creek Cutoff begins southwest of Mesa Lake.

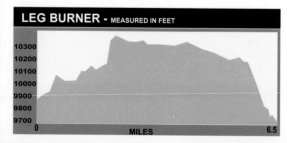

Mileage Estimate

0.0-2.75m Begin this trail south along Mesa Lake and make a right (W) onto the Deep Creek Cutoff trail. Continue this as it turns into Deep Creek and trek uphill and atop the Mesa to Anderson Reservoirs #1 and #2.

2.75-5.25m Cross Anderson Reservoir Road to the DT trail through the trees and open fields down to the historical cabins.

5.25-6.5m Cross eastward over Lands End Road to the south side of the Mesa. Drop down into a steep section and to the Coal Creek junction and the end of the trail.

6.5-13.0m Turn around or continue on Coal Creek.

Trail Description: Deep Creek/Cutoff is a trail that winds past several lakes and reservoirs through some heavily forested terrain. This beautiful scenery makes this trail ideal for families, with lots of places to stop for fishing or skipping rocks. Many different kinds of wildlife such as bears, elk, deer, and birds make their homes in the surrounding areas. The abundance of water in the area can mean having to trek through some marshy areas, so bringing extra socks and bug spray is always a good idea. At the end of the trail, you can make a side trip to Carson Lake by taking the trail off to the left (E).

LEG BURNER - MEASURED IN FEET

MILES		
10300		
10200		
10100		
10000		
9900		
9800		
9700		
0		6.5

Your Local Banking Partner

326 Main Street • Downtown
2415 F Road • Mesa Mall
2257 Broadway • Redlands

241-9000

THE BANK
OF GRAND JUNCTION

www.bogj.com

Mesa Lakes Shore to Lost Lake - Grand Mesa

Distance: 2.8 one way/ 4.8 mile out and back
Elevation Gain: 550 feet   **Use:** Moderate
Foot Difficulty: Easy

Trail Location: Around 45 miles from Grand Junction, east on I-70. Take Exit #49 and turn right (S) on State Hwy 65. Go 25 miles to Mesa Lakes Resort. Turn right (SE) and park near the Mesa Lakes restaurant.

East

Trail Description: Mesa Lakes is a beautiful trail that journeys through boulder fields and wildflower covered meadows. It is a gentle ST climb to several crystal clear lakes that are ideal for fishing, picnicking, painting, or just plain gazing. There are delightful things such as wild strawberries, beaver dams, and even some jumping fish. All of this makes this a great trail for families and dogs.

Mileage Estimate

0.0-0.3m Start out of the parking area by Mesa Lakes. Follow the dirt road to the paved road. Then turn left (E) on the trail.

0.3-1.3m Circle Mesa Lake through the pine forests and boulder field, then left (S) to South Mesa Lake via Lost Lake.

1.3-2.8m Follow the trail around South Mesa Lake and continue up some moderate switchbacks to the sparkling green Lost Lake.

2.8-4.8m Turn around or continue on Deep Creek Cutoff.

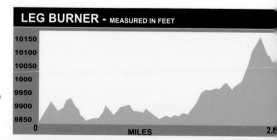

LEG BURNER - MEASURED IN FEET

10150	
10100	
10050	
1000	
9950	
9900	
9850	

0   MILES   2.8

Powderhorn Mountain Road - Ski Resort

Distance: 3.1 miles one way/ 6.2 miles out and back
Elevation Gain: 1,650 feet
Foot Difficulty: Moderate-Difficult
Use: Heavy-winter/Light-summer
Biking Difficulty: Moderate-Difficult

Trail Location: access 1 Powderhorn Ski Area is located 35 miles outside of Grand Junction. Take I-70 to Exit #49, then go south on State Hwy 65 for 20 miles to the Powderhorn Ski Area Sign. Turn right (W) and follow the road 1 mile to the parking area. The Powderhorn Mountain Road begins at the bottom just left/east of Take Four Lift. Or at the top of the ski area behind the same lift.
access 2 Just over 2.5 miles along West Bench at the Take Four Lift.

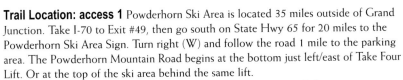

East

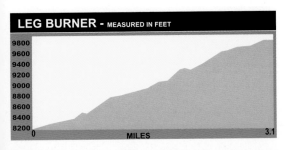

Mileage Estimate

0.0-3.1m Start this 5K uphill trail just left (E) of the Take Four Lift. The trail switchbacks between the ski runs. The DT service road can get steep at times and is quite wet during the spring and early summer with small streams crossing the road. At the top, it meets up with West Bench.

Trail Description: Although you can trek up any ski trail you like all year round, the main service road that heads to the top is the most popular, especially in the summer and fall. Extend your journey directly south on West Bench in any direction. There is plenty of wildlife and plants to identify along both routes. There are plenty of paths for your favorite wintertime activity as well.

3.1-6.2m Return the same way you came for a supreme 10K run or continue either direction along West Bench.

LEG BURNER - MEASURED IN FEET

9800
9600
9400
9200
9000
8800
8600
8400
8200
0   MILES   3.1

West Bench #501 - Grand Mesa National Forest

Distance: 6.5 miles one way/ 13 miles out and back
Elevation Gain: 850 feet   **Use:** Moderate
Foot Difficulty: Easy-Moderate   **Biking Difficulty:** Easy-Moderate

Trail Location: East out of Grand Junction on I-70 to Exit #49. Turn right (S) on State Hwy 65 and go 25 miles to Jumbo Reservoir near the Mesa Lakes Resort. Turn right (W) and follow the road and park at the Mesa Lakes Park Ranger Station next to Sunset Lake Dam. West Bench starts in front of the ranger stations and across from the dam.

East

Mileage Estimate

0.0-0.2m The trail starts to the right (W) near the group of cabins.

0.2-2.6m Drop downhill onto the ST, through the rocky section, and a series of ups and downs until reaching the first ski lift just south of Powderhorn.

2.6-5.0m Continue through the aspens and pines, contending with a few rocky areas and creek crossings to the second chair lift south of the Powderhorn Ski Area.

5.0-6.5m After the second ski lift and the gate, turn left (S). Follow the DT to the top of the Mesa.

6.5-13.0m Turn around or continue to the dirt road and up to Anderson Reservoir Road and loop your way back.

Trail Description: West Bench is a very popular and wide ST that travels through the forest and along a bench just above the Powderhorn Ski Area. It is not really difficult, so even little children can enjoy this trail. Many kinds of wildlife like deer, elk, and birds can be seen in the area. In the summertime, this trail is a pleasant way to escape the heat.

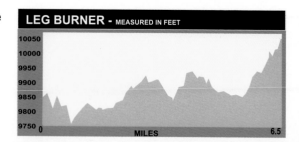

LEG BURNER - MEASURED IN FEET

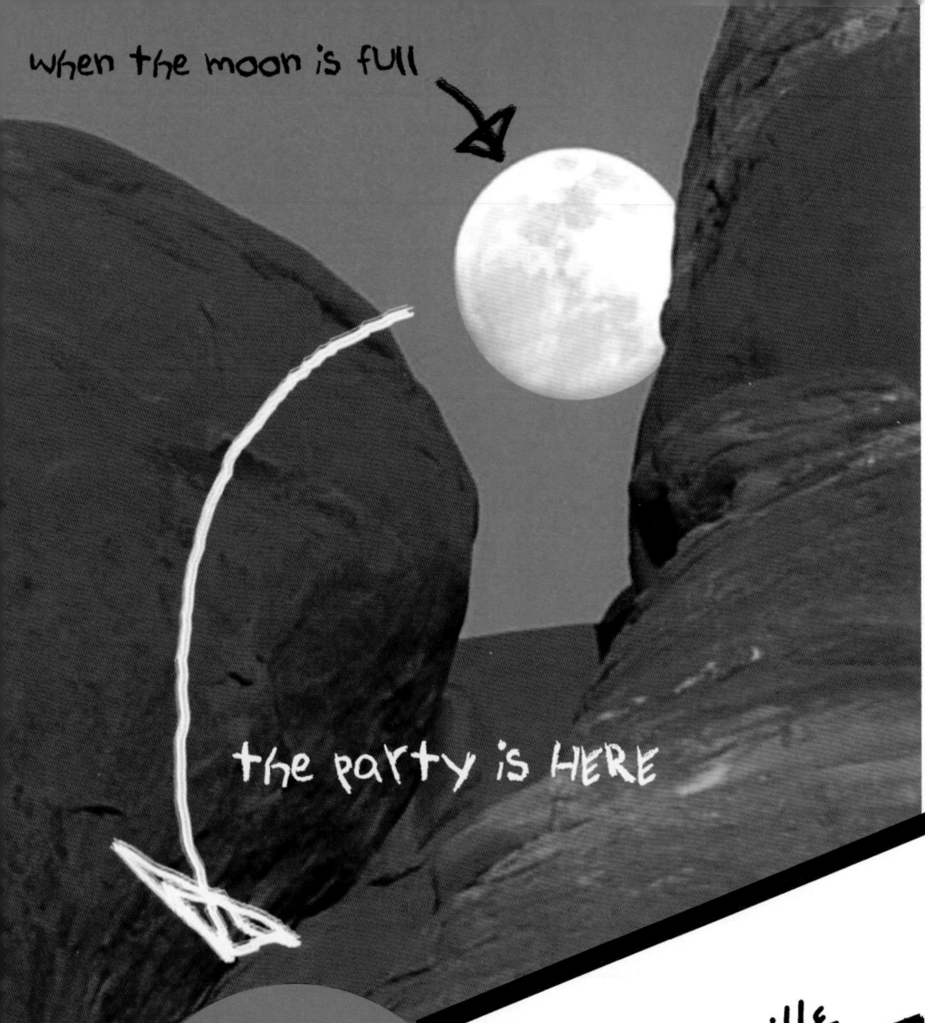
when the moon is full
the party is HERE

The Grand Mesa Visitor Center

10240

P
P

Cottonwood
Lake No 1

Cottonwood
Lake No 4

10660

11085

d Sore

MESA   CO
DELTA   CO

hiking only

10660

36

Upper Hotel
Lake

Upper Eggleston
Lake

Arch
Slough

Hotel
Lake

P Campgrou

FR 121

Grand
Mesa

FR 121

FR 121

Eggleston ▲ Campground
Lake

Alexand

FR 121

P

P ▲

Deep Ward
Lake

Huron
Lake

6   Donnely
Res

Kiser
Res

Ryan
Res

Deep Slough
Res

Kennicott
Slough Res

FR 123

Womack
Res No 2

Kiser
Slough Res

10040

9940

Spring

9840

9020

748   p 170 Ward Creek
oods   p 170 Ward Lake #744
9

OutdoorGuru.com

© 2002 OutdoorGuru.com & ✕ MAPTECH
These maps or any portion thereof may not be reproduced

Bull Creek Reservoir #507 - Grand Mesa National Forest

Distance: 4.9 miles one way/ 9.8 miles out and back
Elevation Gain: 525 feet/ 400 feet   **Use:** Moderate
Foot Difficulty: Easy-Moderate   **Biking Difficulty:** Moderate

Trail Location: access 1 East out of Grand Junction on I-70 to Exit #49. Turn right (S) on State Hwy 65. Just after State Hwy 65 makes a hard right (SW) at 28 miles, turn left (NE). Follow the dirt road a half mile to the parking area and the Lake of the Woods West Trailhead. Bull Creek Reservoir Trail begins 5 miles along Lake of the Woods.
access 2 Around 20 miles south of Collbran on 59 Road which becomes FR 121. Turn right (SW) on FR 257 and go just over 4 miles to the Cottonwood Lake Parking Area and the Lake of the Woods East Trailhead. Bull Creek Reservoir begins 1 miles along Lake of the Woods.

East

Mileage Estimate (starting from access 1)

0.0-0.5m Go northwest to the path that heads to Cottonwood Lake #2.

0.5-2.0m Turn left (SW) away from this path.

2.0-3.0m The trail turns right (W) and goes around Bull Creek Reservoir #2

3.0-4.9m After passing Bull Creek Reservoir, make your way west to maintained road to the end of the road and the Bull Creek Reservoir junction.

4.9-9.8m Continue on Bull Creek Cutoff and Lake of the Woods or head back.

Trail Description: Bull Creek Reservoir is a DT to the northwest of Lake Woods Trail and is frequently soggy in the lowland depressions near the 5 lakes that are along this trail. To see these lakes, it is necessary to venture off the main path. The mosquitoes can be thick in these areas.

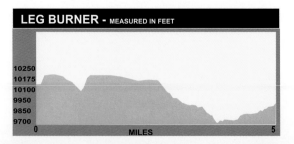

LEG BURNER - MEASURED IN FEET

10250
10175
10100
9950
9850
9700
0   MILES   5

Bull Creek Res. Cutoff #506.1 - Grand Mesa National Forest

Distance: 1.7 miles one way/ 3.4 miles out and back
Elevation Gain: 100 feet/ 325 feet   **Use:** Moderate
Foot Difficulty: Easy-Moderate   **Biking Difficulty:** Moderate

Trail Location: East out of Grand Junction on I-70 to Exit #49. Turn right (S) on State Hwy 65. Just after State Hwy makes a hard right (SW) at 28 miles, turn left (NE). Follow the dirt road a half mile to the parking area and the Lake of the Woods West Trailhead. Bull Creek Reservoir Cutoff is 1.2 miles along Lake of the Woods.

East

Mileage Estimate

0.0-0.7m   Go north and uphill from Lake of the Woods to Bull Creek Reservoir #4.

0.7-1.7m   Trek along on the old DT next to the shore of the lake and downhill to the end of the trail and the Bull Creek Reservoir junction.

1.7-3.4m   Head back or turn right (NE) to continue on Bull Creek Reservoir.

Trail Description: Bull Creek Reservoir Cutoff is a short trail that leads to some excellent fishing spots. It links Lake of the Woods to Bull Creek Reservoir.

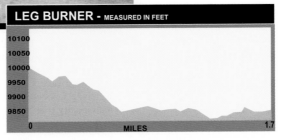

LEG BURNER - MEASURED IN FEET

| 10100 |
| 10050 |
| 10000 |
| 9950 |
| 9900 |
| 9850 |
| 0 | MILES | 1.7 |

Cobbett Lake #747 - Grand Mesa National Forest

Distance: 1 mile one way/ 2 miles out and back
Elevation Gain: 35 feet   **Use:** Heavy
Foot Difficulty: Easy

Trail Location: East out of Grand Junction on I-70 to Exit #49. Turn right (S) on State Hwy 65 for 35 miles to the Visitor Center. Cobbett Lake starts across the road from the Visitor Center.

Trail Description: Cobbett Lake and Cobbett To Ward overlap each other on the way to the Cobbett Campground. It wraps around Cobbett Lake and meets up with Ward Lake, Crag to Cobbett, and Island Lake. It is a great family hike with lots of interesting sights.

East

Cobbett to Ward #746 - Grand Mesa National Forest

Distance: 1 mile one way
              2 miles out and back
Elevation Gain: 25 feet
Use: Heavy
Foot Difficulty: Easy

Trail Location: East out of Grand Junction on I-70 to Exit #49. Turn right (S) on State Hwy 65 for 35 miles to the Visitor Center.

Mileage Estimate

0.0-0.5m From the Visitor Center, go through the trees along the shore of Cobbett Lake to the campground.

0.5-1.0m The trail passes the Matt Arch Slough and then makes its way to Ward Lake where it crosses over 121 Road to the end of the trail.

1.0-2.0m Head back or continue on Cobbett to Ward.

Trail Description: Cobbett To Ward heads to the beautiful Cobbett Lake and Matt Arch Slough lake on the flatlands and over some hills. There is plenty of shade as well as soggy wetlands. Add one of many nearby trails, such as Ward Lake, Crag To Cobbett, Island Lake, and/or Cobbett Lake to spice up a day or multiple day trip.

MLS.
HILL & HOLMES
Real Estate
A FULL SERVICE REAL ESTATE COMPANY
241-SOLD 241-7653
1204 N. 7TH, GRAND JUNCTION, CO.

Cottonwood # 712.1 - Grand Mesa National Forest

Distance: 1.7 miles one way/ 3.4 miles out and back
Elevation Gain: 150 feet/ 600 feet   **Use:** Moderate
Foot Difficulty: Easy-Moderate   **Biking Difficulty:** Moderate

Trail Location: access 1 East out of Grand Junction on I-70 to Exit #49. Turn right (S) on State Hwy 65 and travel 34 miles to a left (N) turn at Crag Crest West Parking Area. Cottonwood begins 1.5 miles along Crag Crest.
access 2 East out of Grand Junction on I-70 to Exit #49. Turn right (S) on State Hwy 65 and travel 28 miles. Just after State Hwy 65 makes a hard right (SW), turn left (NE) onto a dirt road. Follow the dirt road a half mile to the parking area and the Lake of the Woods Trailhead. Cottonwood begins 4.8 miles on the Lake of the Wood.

East

Mileage Estimate (starting from access 1)
0.0-0.7m   Turn left (N) from the Crag Crest/Cottonwood junction.

0.7-1.7m   Follow the steep trail that is covered with roots and rocks to the Lake of the Woods junction.

1.7-2.0m   Continue on Lake of the Woods or Bull Reservoir. To return on Cottonwood stay left (SE).

2.0-3.4m   Continue on to Crag Crest.

Trail Description: Cottonwood is a charming ST that connects Crag Crest to Lake of the Woods and has a top elevation height of 10,880 feet. It is a superb mountain biking trail, providing the only way to get extra miles if you're biking Lower Crag Crest. When returning on Cottonwood, there is a faint trail off to the right at the 2.0 mile mark. This path heads up to Cold Sore Reservoir and it will disappear before it reaches the lake.

LEG BURNER - MEASURED IN FEET

10800		
10700		
10600		
10500		
10400		
10300		
	0	MILES	1

County Line - Grand Mesa National Forest

Distance: 0.75 mile loops to 4.5 mile loops
Elevation Gain: Light   **Use:** Moderate
Skiing Difficulty: Easy-Moderate

Trail Location: East from Grand Junction on I-70. Take Exit #49 and turn right (S) on State Hwy 65. Follow State Hwy 65 for 32 miles just past the Lands End turn off and park in the area on the left side/east of the road.

East

Trail Description: County Line is a series of 4 to 6 loops along the southern end of the Grand Mesa. It was the first group of cross-country ski trails for the National Recreation Trail System. With all of these varying trails, there are several places along the way with spectacular views of the Uncompahgre Plateau, the San Juan Mountains, and the West Elk Mountains. Don't miss out on the Microwave Tower near the end of Loop 3. Skyway can be accessed from this trail. In the spring and summer months, you can hike or bike on County Line, but remember that it is primarily a cross country ski trail, so there are no hiking or biking trail markers.

Crag Crest #711 (upper & lower) - Grand Mesa National Forest

Distance: 10 mile loop
Elevation Gain: 1,850 feet
Foot Difficulty: Moderate

Use: Heavy
Biking Difficulty: Moderate

Trail Location: access 1 East from Grand Junction on I-70. Take Exit #49 and turn right (S) on State Hwy 65. Follow State Hwy 65 for 34 miles and take a left (N) into the West Crag Crest Parking Area.
access 2 From Exit #49 off I-70, travel 35 miles to the Visitor Center and turn left/east onto FR 121. Follow this for about 4 miles to the East Crag Crest Trailhead next to Eggleston Lake.

East

Mileage Estimate (starting from access 1)

0.0-1.0m Go east from the parking area and climb a gentle incline along a maintained ST through the trees and to the Lower Crag Crest junction.

1.0-1.5m Continue straight (NE) and follow the trail up the steep section of switchbacks to Cottonwood junction.

1.5-2.5m Veer right (E) and up the mountain to the first long and narrow crag/ridge.

2.5-4.5m Trek up and down and be careful along this narrow track between the sharp drop-offs on either side.

4.5-6.5m The trail descends to Bullfinch Reservoir #1 and Upper Eggleston Lake and the East Crag Crest junction.

6.5-9.0m Veer right (W) along the Lower Crag Crest, up the steady incline, across the mountain and to the creek just below Forest Lake and the end of Lower Crag Crest.

9.0-10.0m Turn left (SW) and back along the maintained ST to the parking area.

Trail Description: Upper Crag Crest is for foot traffic only because of the elevation and the sheer drop offs on both sides of the trail. For mountain biking and horseback riding, it is easiest to park at East Crag Crest Trailhead and get on Cottonwood and then Lake of the Woods. Lower Crag Crest goes past a couple of pretty lakes, but Upper Crag Crest is the highest trail point on the Grand Mesa, so the views here are spectacular. There are other majestic views of the depressions of lava rock that helped form the Grand Mesa area.

LEG BURNER - MEASURED IN FEET

Try something different...

Choose from local wines to
imported micro brews–at
Cottonwood Liquors there
is always something
different to try.

Cottonwood
LIQUORS

2513 US Hwy 6 & 50
Grand Junction, CO
(970) 243-1062

Crag to Cobbett #749 - Grand Mesa National Forest

Distance: 0.6 miles one way/ 1.2 miles out and back
Elevation Gain: 160 feet   **Use:** Heavy
Foot Difficulty: Easy

Trail Location: East out of Grand Junction on I-70 to Exit #49. Turn right (S) on State Hwy 65 for 35 miles to the Visitor Center.

Trail Description: Crag to Cobbett is a short trail with a moderate elevation change through pine and spruce trees to Crag Crest.

Mileage Estimate

0.0-0.6m   Leave the Visitor Center to the north between Cobbett Lake and Hwy 65 along Cobbett Lake. Cross the dirt road and trek through the trees to Crag Crest.

0.6-1.2m   Head back or continue along Crag Crest.

East

Island Lake #748 - Grand Mesa National Forest

Distance: 1.6 miles one way/ 3.2 miles out and back
Elevation Gain: 100 feet   **Use:** Moderate
Foot Difficulty: Easy

Trail Location: East out of Grand Junction on I-70 to Exit #49. Turn right (S) onto State Hwy 65 for 32.5 miles. Take a right (S) turn at the Island Lake sign. Follow this road to the trailhead and the parking area.

Mileage Estimate

0.0-1.6m   Go through the trees and alongside the beautiful Island Lake.

1.6-3.2m   Head back or cross the road and continue on Cobbett Lake or Cobbett to Crag Crest.

Trail Description: Island Lake has minimal change in elevation and is an enjoyable trail for the whole family. The lake that shares its name with the trail is a great fishing spot.

Lake of the Woods #506 - Grand Mesa National Forest

Distance: 6 miles one way/ 12 miles out and back
Elevation Gain: 650 feet/ 500 feet   **Use:** Moderate
Foot Difficulty: Easy-Moderate   **Biking Difficulty:** Moderate

Trail Location: access 1 East out of Grand Junction on I-70 to Exit #49. Turn right (S) on State Hwy 65. Just after State Hwy makes a hard right (SW) at 28 miles, turn left (NE). Follow the dirt road a half mile to the parking area and the Lake of the Woods West Trailhead. Bull Creek Reservoir Trail begins 5 miles along Lake of the Woods.
access 2 Around 20 miles south of Collbran on 59 Road which becomes FR 121. Turn right (SW) on FR 257 and go just over 4 miles to the Cottonwood Lake Parking Area and the Lake of the Woods East Trailhead. Bull Creek Reservoir begins 1 mile along Lake of the Woods.

East

Mileage Estimate (starting from access 1)

0.0-0.6m   Go east from the parking lot and downhill to the meadow.

0.6-1.2m   Go through the meadow and back out to the Bull Creek Reservoir Cutoff junction.

1.2-1.8m   Turn right (E) uphill and then descend to Bull Basin Reservoir #1. Look right (SE) for the trail. If you reach the shoreline, you have gone too far so backtrack to the trail junction.

1.8-2.5m   Continue along the trail, cross the creek and uphill to the dam and the Bull Creek Reservoir #1.

2.5-4.8m   Continue along the left (N) shore of Bull Creek and follow the trail to the open grassland at the highest elevation then go down to the Cottonwood junction.

Trail Description: Lake of the Woods meanders through the trees and sometimes wet meadows on the way to and around several lakes. A great loop can be made with Bull Creek Reservoir Cutoff. If you continue past the east parking area you can go out to Lilly Lake for a short side trip.

4.8-6.0m   Continue east, passing Bull Creek Reservoir to the left (NW) and follow the north side of Cottonwood Lake #1. The trail ends just past the dam at the parking area.

6.0-12.0m   Head back or continue along Lilly Lake.

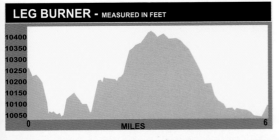

LEG BURNER - MEASURED IN FEET

10400
10350
10300
10250
10200
10150
10100
10050
0   MILES   6

Distance: 3.5 mile loops to 15 mile loops
Elevation Gain: Light   **Use:** Moderate
Skiing Difficulty: Easy-Moderate

Trail Location: East from Grand Junction on I-70. Take Exit #49 and turn right (S) on State Hwy 65. Follow State Hwy 65 for 29 miles just before the Lands End Road turn off and park in the area on the left/east side of the road.

East

Trail Description: The loops that make up the Skyway Trail loop through groves of trees and across open areas. Whiteout conditions can occur in these wide open areas, so be prepared. An overlook located along the north section of the trail has a majestic view of the Book Cliffs and the mountains in the northern boundary of the Grand Mesa National Forest north of Collbran. Skyway Trail links to the Sunset Trail and County Line.

Ward Lake #744 - Grand Mesa National Forest

Distance: 1.2 miles one way/ 2.4 miles out and back
Elevation Gain: 0 feet　　　　**Use:** Heavy
Foot Difficulty: Easy

Trail Location: East out of Grand Junction on I-70 to Exit #49. Turn right (S) on State Hwy 65 for 35 miles to the Visitor Center. Ward Lake is a half mile east of the Visitor Center along 121 Road.

Mileage Estimate

0.0-1.2m This trail follows next to the shoreline of Ward Lake and connects Cobbett to Ward Trail across the road.

1.2-2.4m Turn around or take the dirt road north along the west shoreline.

Trail Description: Ward Lake is a good family trail and is a great place to fish, camp, picnic or stop in at the Visitor Center where it joins up with Cobbett Lake and Cobbett To Ward.

East

Ward Creek - Grand Mesa National Forest

Distance: 1.5 mile loops to 10 mile loops
Elevation Gain: Light　　　　**Use:** Moderate
Skiing Difficulty: Moderate-Difficult

Trail Location: access 1 East out of Grand Junction on I-70 to Exit #49. Turn right (S) on State Hwy 65 for 36 miles to the Visitor Center.

Trail Description: The Ward Creek series of trail loops travel near and around several bodies of water, including Ward Creek and Ward Lake through the pines and aspens and mountain meadows. These open mountain meadows offer fantastic views of the San Juan Mountains and the West Elk Mountains. If you park at the parking lot near the Visitor Center, keep in mind that the trek back up is difficult and it will take at least twice as much time as going down. You can also access Ward Creek from Ward Creek Reservoir, or from Spruce Lodge or Alexander Lake Lodge.

The Grand Mesa Vega State Park

Bogue Mountain 8970
McKenzie Res
voir
7380
9130 Baldridge Point
8200
9300 Two Peak
9020
9970 Porter Mountain
9020
9020
TRAIL
PACK
Pidreaty
2023
P
9840
NATIONAL FOREST
9840
9840
Branco Knob
10120
9840
MESA
The Flat
36
10690
PACK
TRAIL
Willow Ridge
10890
NATIONAL FOREST BOUNDARY
Creek
Ranger
Fremont
Creek
Creek
Tops
10660
9840
Monument Res No 2
P
11150 Chalk Mountain
TRAIL
Duke
P
Creek
PACK
TRAIL
Monument Res No-1
10660
10660
9840
Calby Horse Park Reservoir
10700
Overland Reservoir
PACK
10810
10940
10660
Hunter Reservoir
10660
Nat For
BDY
11310 Mt Hatten
Main
Hubba
Gaging Stations
36
36
Priest Mtn
Middle
10980
11330 Crater Peak
Dogfish Res
Goodenough Reservoir
Middle
Reynolds Res
Elk Res
11310 Mt Darline
10660
Gaging Sta
Thickle Res
Hanson Res
Bailey Res
9840
Hilltop Res
Willow Reservoir
West
10660
Sioux Creek
9740
P
Willow Creek
10930

East Leon #730 - Grand Mesa National Forest

Distance: 9.5 miles one way/ 19 miles out and back
Elevation Gain: 1,100 feet/ 1,100 feet   **Use:** Moderate
Foot Difficulty: Easy-Difficult   **Biking Difficulty:** Moderate-Difficult

Trail Location: access 1 East from Grand Junction on I-70 to Exit #49. Turn right (S) onto State Hwy 65 for 10 miles. Then turn left/east on State Hwy 330 and go 18 miles through Collbran. Make a right (SE) at the Y intersection onto 64.6 Road. Follow the road for 3 miles up to the Vega State Recreation Area entrance station. From the entrance station, continue a short distance up the road and turn right (S), cross the dam and pass the Visitor Center. Turn right (S) onto 66.60 Road which becomes into FR 262 and then it becomes FR 280. The East Leon begins 9 miles up the dirt road from the 66.60 Road turn off. **access 2** See Elk Park access on page 183.

East

LEG BURNER - MEASURED IN FEET

Mileage Estimate

0.0-1.25m Head southeast along the rocky DT up to a group of trees where the trail plateaus.

1.25-4.7m The trail weaves in and out of the trees, down to the grassland, and then through a couple of creeks. Go uphill to the Mesa/Delta County fence line.

4.7-7.7m Continue downhill to Marshy Park and the Elk Park junction.

7.7-9.5m Continue south and down the DT to the end of the trail and the southern access.

9.5-19.0m Head back to the north and the parking area.

Trail Description: East Leon is a DT that goes to the top of the Grand Mesa, passing by Priest Mountain which is the highest peak in the area. It travels through trees and open meadows from one side of the Grand Mesa National Forest to the other and has a top elevation of 10,650 feet.

High Trail #515 - Grand Mesa National Forest

Distance: 9.2 miles one way/ 18.4 miles out and back
Elevation Gain: 1,350 feet/ 1,600 feet   **Use:** Moderate
Foot Difficulty: Easy-Difficult   **Biking Difficulty:** Moderate-Difficult

Trail Location: East from Grand Junction on I-70 to Exit #49. Turn right (S) onto State Hwy 65 for 10 miles. Then turn left/east on State Hwy 330 and go 18 miles through Collbran. Make a right (SE) at the Y intersection onto 64.6 Road. Follow the road for 3 miles up to the Vega State Recreation Area entrance station. From the entrance station, continue a short distance up the road and turn right (S), cross the dam and pass the Visitor Center. Turn right (S) onto 66.60 Road which becomes FR 262 and then FR 280. Park at the trailhead up the road 6.8 miles on the left/east.

East

Trail Description: High Trail travels along a DT through the trees and near a lot of boggy areas. The Flat Tops area is the trail's top elevation of 10,650 feet.

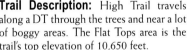

LEG BURNER - MEASURED IN FEET

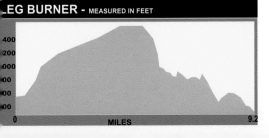

Mileage Estimate

0.0-4.8m Climb sharply up through the aspen trees to the Flat Tops area.

4.8-6.3m Travel across the Flat Tops and down to Stillwater Park and Plateau Creek.

6.3-9.2m Continue along the creek through the trees, and veer right (E) with the trail over the open meadow and to the end of the trail.

9.2-18.4m This trail can be a 2 day trek or a serious single day out and back.

Monument #518 - Grand Mesa National Forest

Distance: 11.2 miles one way/ 22.4 miles out and back
Elevation Gain: 1,200 feet/ 1,400 feet   **Use:** Moderate
Foot Difficulty: Easy-Difficult   **Biking Difficulty:** Moderate-Difficult

Trail Location: East from Grand Junction on I-70 to Exit #49. Turn right (S) onto State Hwy 65 for 10 miles. Then turn left/east on State Hwy 330 and go 18 miles through Collbran. Make a right (SE) at the Y intersection onto 64.6 Road. Follow the road for 3 miles up to the Vega State Recreation Area entrance station. From the entrance station, continue a short distance up the road and turn right (S), cross the dam and pass the Visitor Center. Turn right (S) onto 66.60 Road which becomes FR 262 and then FR 280. Park at the trailhead 7.8 miles up the road.

East

Mileage Estimate

0.0-2.9m Follow along the north side of Monument Creek uphill through the grasslands to Monument Reservoir #1 and the turn off to Monument Reservoir #2.

2.9-5.5m The trail levels out and curves more gently through the trees.

5.5-11.2m Follow the trail down and across the upper portion of Plateau Creek. Continue down and through Willow Creek Park, passing the Buzzard Creek Trail junction and Wagon Park to the end of the trail at FR Road 263.

11.2-22.4m Head back or camp in Wagon Park.

Trail Description: Monument is an extremely long trail up to the top of the Flat Tops Area and down to Wagon Park. It has splendid views of Monument Reservoir #1 and can make a long loop with the High Trail.

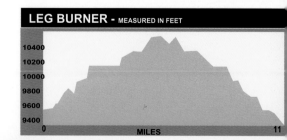

LEG BURNER - MEASURED IN FEET

10400
10200
10000
9800
9600
9400
0   MILES   11

Salt Creek #514 - Grand Mesa National Forest

Distance: 6.4 miles one way/ 12.8 miles out and back
Elevation Gain: 2,000 feet/ 600 feet   **Use:** Moderate
Foot Difficulty: Easy-Difficult   **Biking Difficulty:** Moderate-Difficult

Trail Location: East from Grand Junction on I-70 to Exit #49. Turn right (S) onto State Hwy 65 for 10 miles. Then turn left/east on State Hwy 330 and go 18 miles through Collbran. Make a right (SE) at the Y intersection onto 64.6 Road. Follow the road for 3 miles up to the Vega State Recreation Area entrance station. From the entrance station, continue a short distance up the road and turn right (S), cross the dam and pass the Visitor Center. Turn right (S) onto 66.60 Road which becomes FR 262 and then FR 280. Park at the trailhead 3.2 miles up the road.

East

Trail Description: Salt Creek is a DT that heads up through some aspen and spruce trees with significant elevation changes. There are awe inspiring views of Collbran from the top of Sheep Flats.

Mileage Estimate

0.0-1.5m Go west, past a small pond and downhill across the creek. Then go north to an easier and more level grade.

1.5-2.2m Now the trail makes a big change and goes sharply uphill to the west and the trail junction that heads down to Salt Creek Road.

2.2-3.4m Turn left (S) uphill over an 800 foot section to the top of Salt Mountain at 9,804 feet.

3.4-5.2m Continue along the top, then back down to the next junction that heads downhill.

5.2-6.4m Veer left (S), go across the creek and to the end of the trail at FR 279.

6.4-12.8m Turn around and head back the way you came.

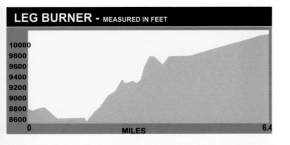

LEG BURNER - MEASURED IN FEET

MILES	
10000	
9800	
9600	
9400	
9200	
9000	
8800	
8600	
0	6.4

Silver Spruce #517 - Grand Mesa National Forest

Distance: 8.6 miles one way/ 17.2 miles out and back
Elevation Gain: 1,850 feet/ 2,200 feet   **Use:** Moderate
Foot Difficulty: Easy-Difficult   **Biking Difficulty:** Moderate-Difficult

Trail Location: East from Grand Junction on I-70 to Exit #49. Turn right (S) onto State Hwy 65 for 10 miles. Then turn left/east on State Hwy 330 and go 18 miles through Collbran. Make a right (SE) at the Y intersection onto 64.6 Road. Follow the road for 3 miles up to the Vega State Recreation Area entrance station. From the entrance station, continue a short distance up the road and turn right (S), cross the dam and pass the Visitor Center. Turn right (S) onto 66.60 Road which becomes FR 262 and then FR 280. Park at the trailhead 4 miles up the road on the left/east hand side.

East

Mileage Estimate

0.0-2.0m Climb sharply up along the narrow DT and steeply up to below Chop Mountain.

2.0-5.4m Follow the trail as it descends and crosses over 3 creeks and then back down again to cross Plateau Creek.

5.4-8.6m Follow along the northern shoulder of Plateau Ridge. The trail ends at the bottom at FR 266.

8.6-17.2m Head back or make a loop with High Trail above.

Trail Description: Silver Spruce goes up and down like a roller coaster to the end of its 8.5 mile one way ride. It has incredible views of Collbran and in some spots you can even glimpse Vega Lake.

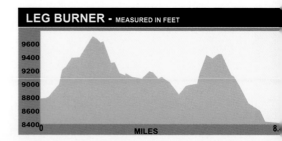

LEG BURNER - MEASURED IN FEET

9600
9400
9200
9000
8800
8600
8400

0   MILES   8.

FRESH

infinite visual innovations

Producing creative solutions in marketing, print, and web design.

MONUMENT GRAPHICS
& communications

p: 970.242.4311 MonumentGraphics.com

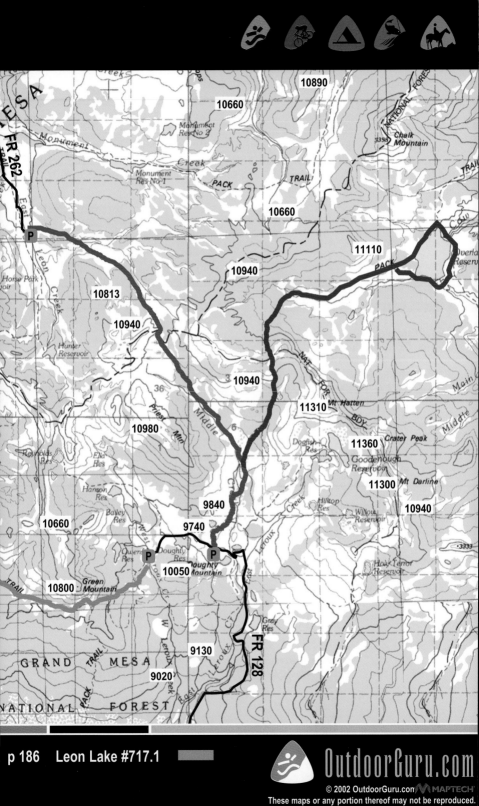

Bonham #512 - Grand Mesa National Forest

Distance: 2.8 miles one way/ 5.6 miles out and back
Elevation Gain: 525 feet   **Use:** Moderate
Foot Difficulty: Easy-Moderate   **Biking Difficulty:** Easy-Moderate

Trail Location: East from Grand Junction on I-70 to Exit #49. Turn right (S) onto State Hwy 65 for 10 miles. Then turn left/east on State Hwy 330 and go 11.2 miles and make a right (S) onto 58.5 Road. Follow 58.5 Road/59 Road for 11.5 miles to FR 259 and turn right (W). Follow this road for 0.7 miles, around Bonham Reservoir, over the dam and to the trailhead on the right (W). Park here.

East

Mileage Estimate

0.0-0.7m Follow the DT trail up through the trees and join the maintained road to the Forest Service only access.

0.7-2.3m Turn right (NW) off the maintained road onto a DT, through the open grassland to the top elevation and the gate.

2.3-2.8m Head downhill from the gate as the trail turns left (S) to FR #258.

2.8-5.6m Turn around for the out and back.

Trail Description: Bonham is a short DT between FR #259 and FR #258 and offers a variety of picture perfect spots, including the area around the lake that can be seen from the ridge along Crag Crest and the surprising sight of the Mesa and the back of the Book Cliffs.

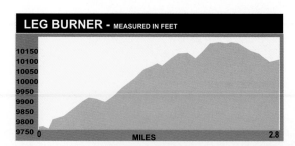

LEG BURNER - MEASURED IN FEET

10150
10100
10050
10000
9950
9900
9850
9800
9750
0   MILES   2.8

Cedar Mesa #718 - Grand Mesa National Forest

Distance: 3.2 miles one way/ 6.4 miles out and back
Elevation Gain: 500 feet/ 700 feet   **Use:** Moderate
Foot Difficulty: Easy-Moderate   **Biking Difficulty:** Moderate

Trail Location: access 1 East out of Grand Junction on I-70 to Exit #49. Turn right (S) on Hwy 65 for 10 miles. Turn left/east on State Hwy 330 for 11.2 miles. Make a right (S) onto 58.5 Road. Follow 58.5/59 Road for 15.5 miles to FR 125. Turn left (S) onto FR 125 and follow this road 1.3 miles to FR 132. Turn left/east onto FR 132 and follow this difficult 4 wheel drive road for 1.3 miles and park at the trailhead.
access 2 3 miles north of Cedaredge to U50 Road. Turn right/east for 1.8 miles to 25.00 Drive. Make a left (N) onto 25.00 Drive and follow this 8.1 miles to FR 132. Turn right/east and park at the trailhead 1.3 miles up the road.

East

Mileage Estimate

0.0-1.5m   From the top of Cedar Mesa Reservoir Dam, follow the trail east and uphill to the Trio Reservoir.

1.5-3.2m   Continue around the reservoir to the top elevation of 10,300 feet and then descend to Cherry Lake and Marcott Road/FR #127 to the end of the trail.

3.2-6.4m   Head back or continue along the Aqueduct Trail off of Marcott Road/FR #127.

Trail Description: Cedar Mesa is a DT up through the spruce trees and a few aspens. It travels to and around several lakes and makes a fun loop with the Aqueduct Trail south and below Cedar Mesa.

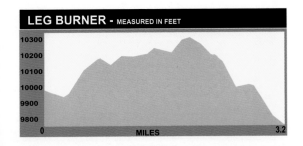

LEG BURNER - MEASURED IN FEET

Elk Park #720 - Grand Mesa National Forest

Distance: 7.35 miles one way/ 14.7 miles out and back
Elevation Gain: 1,200 feet/ 1,100 feet   **Use:** Moderate
Foot Difficulty: Easy-Difficult   **Biking Difficulty:** Moderate-Difficult

Trail Location: This trail is located around 75 miles from Grand Junction. Leave Grand Junction to the south on Highway 50 to Delta. After entering Delta, turn left/east at Highway 92 toward Hotchkiss. Then turn left (N) just before you reach Hotchkiss on 31.00 Road. Follow this road for 19 miles as the road becomes FR 128. Make a left (NW) at 1b Road and park 0.7 miles up the road. Elk Park begins 1.8 miles along East Leon on the southern trailhead location.

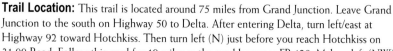

East

Mileage Estimate

0.0-2.1m From the East Leon junction, head northeast through the open grassland and then suddenly moves into the trees and rises steeply up to the National Forest border and the top elevation of 10,800 feet.

2.1-5.4m Follow the trail into the Gunnison National Forest and then down to Elk Park and Overland Reservoir.

5.4-9.3m Go either direction, as the trail loops around the reservoir.

9.3-14.7m Head back to the parking area.

Trail Description: Elk Park is a DT that travels through the Grand Mesa and Gunnison forests. It has amazing views of Elk Park, Overland Reservoir, and the Gunnison National Forest.

LEG BURNER - MEASURED IN FEET

10600
10400
10200
10000
9800

0   MILES   9.3

Eureka #734/Cutoff #734.1 Loop - Grand Mesa

Distance: 8.25 mile loop
Elevation Gain: 1,025 feet   **Use:** Moderate
Foot Difficulty: Easy-Moderate   **Biking Difficulty:** Moderate

Trail Location: access 1 3 miles north of Cedaredge to U50 Road. Turn right (E) onto U50 Road and go 1.8 miles and turn left (NE) onto 25.00 Drive. Follow this road for 8 miles and make a left (W) onto FR 125.1a. Park at the Eureka Trailhead a short distance up the road.

access 2 10 miles north of Cedaredge to FR 123. Turn right (N) onto FR 123 and veer right (NE) onto FR 129. Follow FR 129 for 2 miles to the West Green Mountain Trailhead. Eureka is 1 mile and Eureka Cutoff is 2 miles along Green Mountain to the left (NE).

Mileage Estimate (starting from access 1)

0.0-1.75m From Trickle Park Reservoir, go south to the top of Eureka Mountain and then quickly down to the Eureka Cutoff junction.

1.75-3.5m Veer right (W) around Hay Park Reservoir #1 and downhill to the Green Mountain junction.

3.5-4.5m Turn left (S) along the DT to Eureka Cutoff junction on the left (SW).

4.5-6.5m Turn left (NE) along Eureka Cutoff, crossing Horse Creek and next to Eureka Reservoir #1 and back to Eureka. This is the end of the loop.

6.5-8.25m Veer right (E) up to Eureka Mountain and back to parking.

Trail Description: Eureka/Cutoff Loop goes around 5 lakes and atop the Grand Mesa, where there are fabulous views of the south valley toward Cedaredge. This grazing land for a large amount of cattle.

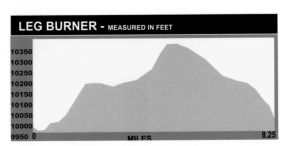

LEG BURNER - MEASURED IN FEET

10350
10300
10250
10200
10150
10100
10050
10000
9950   0   MILES   8.25

Green Mountain #719 - Grand Mesa National Forest

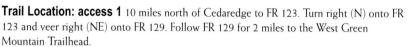

Distance: 13 miles one way/ 26 miles out and back
Elevation Gain: 1,800/ 2,200 feet   **Use:** Moderate
Foot Difficulty: Easy-Difficult   **Biking Difficulty:** Easy-Difficult

Trail Location: access 1 10 miles north of Cedaredge to FR 123. Turn right (N) onto FR 123 and veer right (NE) onto FR 129. Follow FR 129 for 2 miles to the West Green Mountain Trailhead.

access 2 3 miles north of Cedaredge to U50 Road. Turn right (E) onto U50 Road and go 1.8 miles and turn left (NE) onto 25.00 Drive. Follow this road for 5 miles and park next to the Green Mountain trail on either side of the road.

access 3 West about 2 miles before Hotchkiss, northward onto 31.00 Road to FR 128 and then the Eastern Green Mountain Trailhead next to Doughty Reservoir.

East

Mileage Estimate (starting from access 1)

0.0-5.0m Begin southeast on a DT, passing Eureka/Eureka Cutoff to the southern face of the Mesa then to FR 125 Road.

5.0-7.0m Cross the road and to the south, the trail joins FR 127 then heads up the road a short distance and veer right (E) at the Triangle Stomp Trailhead.

7.0-13.0m Continue east around the base of Green Mountain and up to FR 128.1 and the end of the trail.

13.0-26.0m Head back or continue on East Leon.

Trail Description: Green Mountain trail is a good moderate DT that meanders through many aspens, showing their many colors during the fall and late summer. You can park at the access 2 area at the half way point of this trail to shorten the out and back. Or camp out anywhere along the way and break up the trail over more than one day. Either way, beware of the large amount of motorized traffic on this trail.

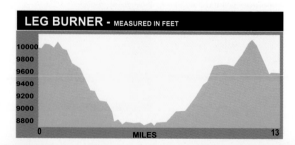

LEG BURNER - MEASURED IN FEET

10000
9800
9600
9400
9200
9000
8800

0   MILES   13

Leon Lake # 717 - Grand Mesa National Forest

Distance: 1.9 miles one way/ 3.8 miles out and back
Elevation Gain: 75 feet/ 150 feet   **Use:** Moderate
Foot Difficulty: Easy   **Biking Difficulty:** Easy-Moderate

Trail Location: Around 65 miles from Grand Junction, east on I-70 to Exit #49. Turn right (S) on State Hwy 65 for 10 miles. Then turn left (E) on State Hwy 330 and go 11.2 miles and make a right (S) at 58.5 Road. Follow 58.5 Road for 14.5 miles and turn left (E) onto FR 126. Park at the Leon Lake and Sissy Trailheads 2.8 miles up the road.

East

Trail Description: Leon Lake is a ST and DT that offers dazzling lake and mountain views on the way through the trees from lake to lake. Take advantage of the commercial campground near Weir and Johnson Reservoir, or anywhere along the trail. A spot near the gorgeous Leon Lake pictured above would certainly add some beauty and calm to the excursion.

Mileage Estimate

0.0-1.0m Travel alongside Weir and Johnson Reservoir then over the first small ridge to Leon Park Reservoir. Then go down to Leon Lake.

1.0-1.9m Turn right (E) just before the shore and make your way along the south side of the lake to FR 127 where the trail ends.

1.9-3.8m Head back to the parking area and try Sissy Trail on the other side of the Weir and Johnson Dam.

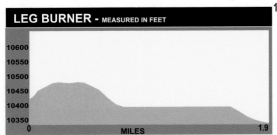

LEG BURNER - MEASURED IN FEET

10600	
10550	
10500	
10450	
10400	
10350	
0	MILES 1.9

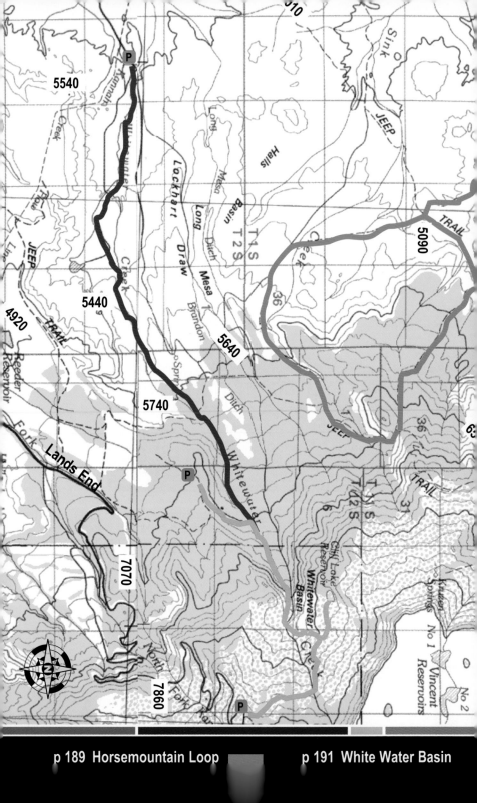

5540

5440

4920

Reeder Reservoir

JEEP   TRAIL

Flow Line

Lockhart Draw

Whitewater   Creek

Long   Ditch

Mesa   T 2 S

Brandon

Spring

Long   Basin

Mesa   Halls

T 1 S   T 2 S

Sink

JEEP   TRAIL

5090

36

Creek

5640

5740

Ditch

JEEP   TRAIL

36

31

T 1 S
T 2 S
6

Lands End

7070

North Fork

7860

Whitewater

Whitewater   Basin

Chli Lake Reservoir

Creek

Vincent   Reservoirs

Kidder   Spring

No 1

No 2

The Grand Mesa
Palisade

OutdoorGuru.com

Horsemountain Loop - Grand Mesa- Palisade

Distance: 14.2 mile loop
Elevation Gain: 2,400 + feet
Foot Difficulty: Moderate

Use: Moderate
Biking Difficulty: Moderate-Difficult

Trail Location: Travel east out of Grand Junction along Highway 6 to Palisade. Pass through downtown Palisade and over the Colorado River to a right (S) on 38 Road. Follow 38 Road for 1.8 miles as it becomes F 1/4 and head west. Turn left (S) on 37 1/4 Road and go 0.25 miles. Turn right (W) on F Road for 0.3 miles and make a left (S) onto an orchard road. Follow this rocky dirt road for 0.7 miles and park here. If you have a 4x4 high clearance vehicle, continue on as far as you can.

East

Mileage Estimate

0.0-1.7m Climb this rocky DT up through a small canyon wash to an overlook of the western slope of the Mesa.

1.7-2.8m Continue down the rocky DT to the first trail junction.

2.8-3,9m Turn left (NE) to where the trail becomes rockier and very steep at the southern base of Horse Mountain.

3.9-6.2m Turn right (S) and begin a long climb up an extremely rocky track to where the trail peaks.

6.2-7.4m The trail turns to the south and begins its descent to the next trail junction.

7.4-9.4m Veer right (SW) and continue the bumpy trek down.

9.4-11.7m Veer right (W) and go a short distance then veer right (NW) and back to where the loop began.

11.7-14.2m Cross the road traveling north up to the overlook and back to the parking.

Trail Description: Horse Mountain loops to the south of Horse Mountain along a rocky trail. As it climbs up to where the trail tops off at the juniper trees, it becomes completely covered in rocks, so making your way around and in between them can take some time. Beware of the ATV traffic all along the trail.

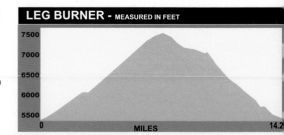

LEG BURNER - MEASURED IN FEET

7500
7000
6500
6000
5500

0   MILES   14.2

Rapid Creek - Grand Mesa -Palisade

Distance: 5 miles one way/ 10 miles out and back
Elevation Gain: 2,250 feet   **Use:** Moderate
Foot Difficulty: Moderate   **Biking Difficulty:** Moderate-Difficult

Trail Location: Northeast out of Grand Junction on Highway 6 to Palisade. Go through Palisade and make a right (E) turn onto 39 5/8 Road. Follow this road north a short distance and make a right (E) turn. Follow this road 1.3 miles to the Cottonwood/Rapid Creek Trailhead.

East

Trail Description: Rapid Creek is very steep, going up 2,000 plus feet in the first 2 miles. It is along the top of the first ridge at the base of the Grand Mesa above Palisade. This rocky DT leads to a series of roads atop the ridge.

Mileage Estimate

0.0-1.5m Climb steeply to the south along a rocky DT until you reach your first trail junction.

1.5-5.0m Turn left (E) to continue the climb to the top of the ridge. You will be entering private property at this time, please be respectful. Trail continues another mile or so downhill to the end of the trail.

5.0-10.0m Turn around and head back, there is nowhere else to continue on from here.

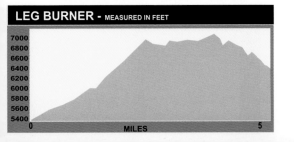

LEG BURNER - MEASURED IN FEET

7000
6800
6600
6400
6200
6000
5800
5600
5400

0   MILES   5

Whitewater Basin #700 - Grand Mesa National Forest

Distance: 4 miles one way/ 8 miles out and back
Elevation Gain: 2,850 feet   **Use:** Light
Foot Difficulty: Moderate-Difficult   **Biking Difficulty:** Difficult

Trail Location: access 1 12 miles south out of Grand Junction on U.S. Hwy 50 to Kannah Creek Road. Turn left (E) and onto Kannah Creek Road for 2.9 miles. Stay straight (E) as the road becomes Lands End Road. Follow Lands End 5.2 miles and turn left (W) onto a dirt road. Follow this road to the creek, where a 4x4 vehicle is needed to drive through the deep water or the dry creek bed. After the creek, go 0.8 miles and turn right (NE) onto a DT. Park anywhere along this road, Whitewater Basin starts at the end of the road.

access 2 From Kannah Creek Road, continue on Lands End Road for 17 miles and park near the trail that begins on the north side.

East

Mileage Estimate (starting from access 1)

0.0-0.8m   Follow the DT along the south side of the creek and look to the right (S) for the partially hidden trail. The DT will dead end a short distance up the hill, so if this happens, simply turn around.

0.8-2.0m   Go right (S) and climb steeply up through the oak brush and the creek uphill along the loose rock to the T split.

2.0-4.0m   Turn right (SE) and go down and back up through another creek to Lands End Road.

4.0-8.0m   Head back this steep downhill back to your car.

Trail Description: Whitewater Basin is a primitive trail up through the oak brush and aspens. The oak brush chokes the trail, making it a narrow path. It can be hard to follow because a large portion of the trail has been eroded by rainfall. At the T split in the trail at 2 miles, you can go left (N) to Cliff Lake to see even more of the picture perfect scenes.

LEG BURNER - MEASURED IN FEET

8860	
8530	
8200	
7870	
7550	
7220	
6890	

0   MILES

Distance: 6.5 miles one way/ 13 miles out and back

Elevation Gain: 1,950 feet   **Use:** Moderate

Foot Difficulty: Moderate-Difficult   **Biking Difficulty:** Moderate-Difficult

Trail Location: South from Grand Junction on US Route 50 for around 8 miles to Whitewater and turn left (E) on Reeder Mesa Road just before the turn off for State Hwy 141. Follow Reeder Mesa Road for 2 miles and make a left (E) onto Whitewater Creek Road. Take this road 2.5 miles to the trailhead on the right (S) side of the road.

East

Trail Description: Whitewater Creek goes through a desert adobe landscape to juniper trees, through the oak brush and toward the aspens and the base of the Grand Mesa and Whitewater Basin. The upper half of the trail is more physically demanding with the increase in elevation through the rocky section. There are BLM trail signs scattered along the trail to make it easier to follow.

LEG BURNER - MEASURED IN FEET

560
230
900
580
250
920

0   MILES   6.5

Mileage Estimate

0.0-1.5m Follow the narrow ST along the north side of the creek and over the ladders on the fence. Cross the creek and head uphill through two gates.

1.5-2.5m Continue on the DT and the south side of the creek to a fence. Parallel this fence line back through the creek to the ST on the right (NE).

2.5-4.0m Follow the ST up through the desert adobe landscape and into some trees. Then go up and over a plateau ridge, passing through a rocky wash to a 4x4 road.

4.0-4.5m Turn right (S) onto this road, to the Y intersection. Turn left (N) and continue up the road for a short distance.

4.5-5.5m Turn right (E) on a narrow DT and follow it uphill, climbing steeply in some spots.

5.5-6.5m The trail turns back into an ST, over the large lava rock, through Whitewater Creek as you make your way to Whitewater Basin.

6.5-13.0m Head back or continue Whitewater Basin.

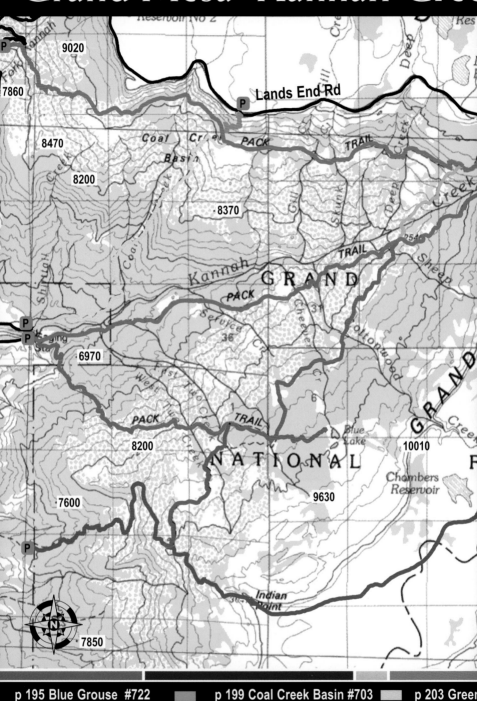

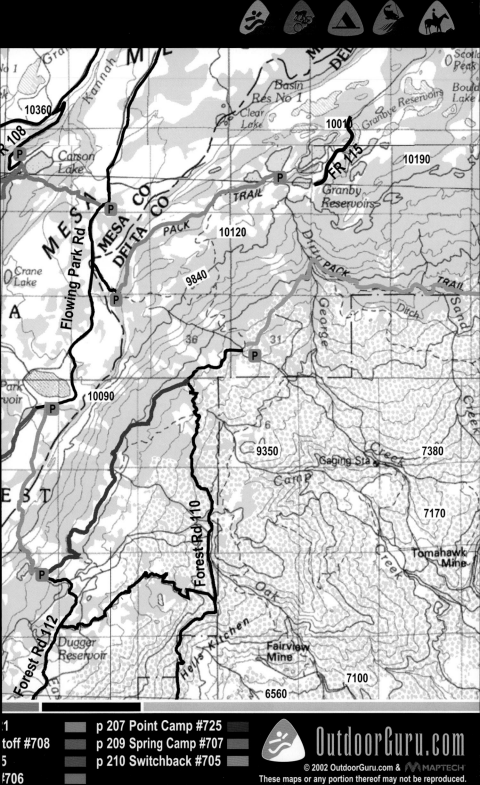

10360

FR 108

P

Carson
Lake

MESA CO

Crane
Lake

Flowing Park Rd

MESA CO
DELTA CO

P

PACK

P

A

Park
Reservoir

P

10090

Forest Rd 112

Dugger
Reservoir

P

Forest Rd 110

Hells Kitchen

Kannah

Basin
Res
No 1

Clear
Lake

TRAIL

P

10120

9840

36

31

6

9350

P

Oak

Fairview
Mine

6560

M   DE

10010

FR 115

Granbye Reservoirs

10190

Granby
Reservoirs

Ditch PACK

George

TRAIL

Sandy

Ditch

Camp

Gaging Sta

Creek

7380

7170

Tomahawk
Mine

Creek

Creek

Fairview
Mine

7100

Scott
Peak

Boul
Lake

p 207 Point Camp #725
p 209 Spring Camp #707
p 210 Switchback #705

Blue Grouse #721 - Grand Mesa National Forest

Distance: 6.4 miles one way/ 12.8 miles out and back
Elevation Gain: 1,150 feet/ 1,400 feet   **Use:** Moderate
Foot Difficulty: Moderate-Difficult   **Biking Difficulty:** Moderate-Difficult

Trail Location: South from Grand Junction on U.S. Hwy 50 to Delta. After reaching Delta, turn left (E) on State Hwy 92. Follow 92 and turn left (NE) onto State Hwy 65. Head north to Eckert to a left (W) onto 19.75 Road, and drive 15 miles. Park here. Begin Blue Grouse from the base of Bull and Brown.

East

Mileage Estimate

0.0-1.6m Travel along a fence line on Road 110 just below the rim of the south face of the Mesa and uphill to Dirty George Creek.

1.6-4.9m Cross the creek and go downhill through a few more creek beds.

4.9-6.4m The trail turns north and heads uphill to the end of the trail and Ward Creek.

6.4-12.8m Head back the way you came and return to your car.

Trail Description: Blue Grouse travels through the aspens and spruce with some stunning mountain and valley vistas of the Cedaredge and Delta area. The section from the parking to the beginning of Bull and Brown is not maintained and has several beaver dams you will have to work your way around.

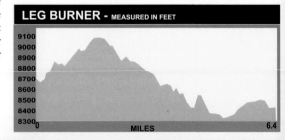

LEG BURNER - MEASURED IN FEET

9100
9000
8900
8800
8700
8600
8500
8400
8300
0   MILES   6.4

Blue Lake #707.1 - Grand Mesa National Forest

Distance: 1 mile one way/ 2 miles out and back
Elevation Gain: 200 feet   **Use:** Light
Foot Difficulty: Easy-Moderate   **Biking Difficulty:** Easy-Moderate

Trail Location: South out of Grand Junction 12 miles on U.S. Hwy 50 through Whitewater to Kannah Creek Road. Turn left (E) and follow the road 2.9 miles. Turn right (SE) and make another quick right (S). Then drive 6.2 miles to Kannah Creek/Spring Camp Parking Area. Blue Lake begins around 4.5 miles along Spring Camp.

East

Mileage Estimate

0.0-1.0m This trail goes to the left (E) off of Spring Camp and can be hard to find.

1.0-2.0m At Blue Lake, turn around. Continue on Spring Camp or return to the car.

Trail Description: Blue Lake makes its way up 200 feet to the little Blue Lake surrounded by thick brush, making it difficult to fish in this lake.

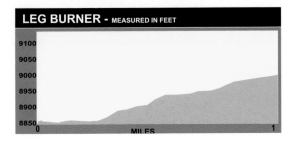

LEG BURNER - MEASURED IN FEET

9100	
9050	
9000	
8950	
8900	
8850	
0	MILES 1

196

Bull and Brown #724 - Grand Mesa National Forest

Distance: 2 miles one way/ 4 miles out and back

Trail Location: East out of Grand Junction on I-70 to Exit #49. Turn right (S) on State Hwy 65 for 31 miles and turn right (SW) onto Lands End Road. Follow Lands End for 1 mile and make a left (SE) onto Flowing Park Road. Continue on Flowing Park for 3.5 miles and turn left (E) onto 1K Road. Park at the Bull and Brown Trailhead a half mile up the road.

East

Trail Description: This trail is temporarily closed for reconstruction.

Carson Lake #729 - Grand Mesa National Forest

Distance: 1.1 miles one way/ 2.2 miles out and back
Elevation Gain: 525 feet   **Use:** Moderate
Foot Difficulty: Easy-Moderate   **Biking Difficulty:** Moderate

Trail Location: East out of Grand Junction on I-70 to Exit #49. Turn right (S) on State Hwy 65 for 31 miles and turn right (SW) onto Lands End Road. Follow Lands End for 2.8 miles and make a left (SE) onto Carson Lake Road. Follow this road and park next to Carson Lake.

Mileage Estimate

0.0-0.2m   Go through the gate below the parking area, cross the dam and to the Kannah Creek junction.

0.2-1.1m   Veer left (SW) and begin climbing up and out of the basin of the lake to the open grassland and a DT road.

1.1-2.2m   Head back or continue on Bull and Brown and Greenwood.

Trail Description: Carson Lake is a short trail from the basin of Carson Lake to the top of the Grand Mesa. At the lake, you can access Kannah Creek and Coal Creek at their upper trailheads. There are several sites for fishing and camping along this trail.

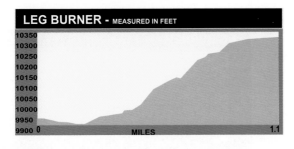

LEG BURNER - MEASURED IN FEET

10350
10300
10250
10200
10150
10100
10050
10000
9950
9900   0   MILES   1.1

Coal Creek #702 - Grand Mesa National Forest

Distance: 9.4 miles one way/ 18.8 miles out and back
Elevation Gain: 2,850 feet   **Use:** Moderate
Foot Difficulty: Moderate   **Biking Difficulty:** Moderate-Difficult

Trail Location: 12 miles south from Grand Junction on U.S. Hwy 50 past Whitewater. Turn left (E) onto Kannah Creek Road. Follow Kannah Creek for 2.9 miles and stay straight (E) as it becomes Lands End Road. Continue for 12.5 miles and turn right (S) into the Wild Rose Picnic Grounds. Park here.

East

Mileage Estimate

0.0-2.2m The trail heads east uphill and climbs an almost 950 foot high rocky section below the rugged wall of the Mesa.

2.2-4.0m Drop down suddenly and then level off through the aspens to the Switchback junction on the left (NE).

4.0-8.0m Continue to the east, passing Coal Creek Basin trail on the right (SE). Continue straight through the trees and open meadows to the very steep climb just before Farmers junction.

8.0-8.4m Look to the right (N) for the trail marker and go uphill to the Deep Creek junction.

8.4-9.4m Continue straight (E) to Carson Lake and the end of the trail.

9.4-18.8m Head back and return to your car.

Trail Description: Coal Creek is a well maintained trail along the northern part of Kannah Creek Basin just below the Mesa's rim. It traverses through the aspens, oak brush, and open meadows with plenty of sunshine. At Farmer's junction, the trail and the land around it has become severely eroded, so be careful.

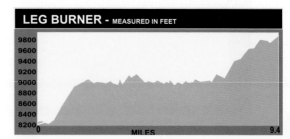

LEG BURNER - MEASURED IN FEET

9800
9600
9400
9200
9000
8800
8600
8400
8200
0   MILES   9.4

Coal Creek Basin #703 - Grand Mesa National Forest

Distance: 5 miles one way/ 10 miles out and back
Elevation Gain: 3,000 feet   **Use:** Moderate
Foot Difficulty: Moderate-Difficult   **Biking Difficulty:** Moderate-Difficult

Trail Location: South out of Grand Junction 12 miles on U.S. Hwy 50 through Whitewater to Kannah Creek Road. Turn left (E) on Kannah Creek and follow the road 2.9 miles. Turn right (SE) and make another quick right (S). Then drive 6.5 mile, passing the Kannah Creek/Spring Camp Parking Area. Park at the Coal Creek Basin Trailhead on the right (N) just past the house.

East

Mileage Estimate

0.0-1.0m Climb up a wide rocky DT that flattens out to an unmarked junction on your left/NE.

1.0-2.5m Turn left (N) onto a wide rocky ST up through the juniper trees to Coal Creek Bridge.

2.5-3.5m Cross the bridge and up the difficult and rocky washed out ST between the oak shrubs.

3.5-5.0m Cross over the portion of the mountainside that has begun to deteriorate and wash away. Find the trail on the other side of this hazardous section to the Coal Creek junction.

5.0-10.0m Head back to the parking area or continue on Coal Creek to Switchback and Carson Lake.

Trail Description: Coal Creek Basin begins at the western base of the Grand Mesa at 6,140 feet and then goes up and over to around 9,000 feet through the juniper forest. The views of the desert floor and the Uncompahgre Plateau are spectacular.

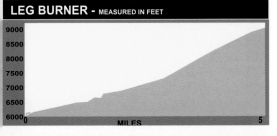

LEG BURNER - MEASURED IN FEET

9000
8500
8000
7500
7000
6500
6000
0   MILES   5

Drop Off #726 - Grand Mesa National Forest

Distance: 2.1 miles one way/ 4.2 miles out and back
Elevation Gain: 25 feet/ 800 feet   **Use:** Moderate
Foot Difficulty: Easy-Difficult   **Biking Difficulty:** Moderate-Difficult

Trail Location: East out of Grand Junction on I-70 to Exit #49. Turn right (S) on State Hwy 65 for 31 miles and turn right (SW) onto Lands End Road. Follow Lands End for 1 mile and turn left (SE) onto Flowing Park Road. Continue Flowing Park for 5.5 miles and park at the Flowing Park Reservoir.

East

Mileage Estimate

0.0-1.2m   The trail crosses an open meadow to the southwest as you approach the rim of the Mesa.

1.2-2.1m   At the rim, follow the rocky switchback down to where the trail plummets almost 700 feet. Follow this steep, loose ST to the Porter Reservoirs.

2.1-4.2m   Head back or continue on Point Camp.

Trail Description: Drop Off does exactly that along the Mesa's southeast side to the Porter Reservoirs and Point Cow Camp Road. Porter Reservoirs is an area with several reservoirs within a half mile of each other, so this trail provides some great fishing spots. It offers spectacular views of the Cedaredge area, the Gunnison National Forest, the southern portion of the Grand Valley and the San Juan Mountains.

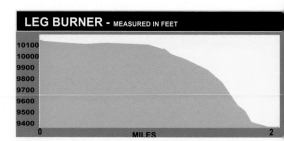

LEG BURNER - MEASURED IN FEET

10100	
10000	
9900	
9800	
9700	
9600	
9500	
9400	

0   MILES   2

Farmer's #727 - Grand Mesa National Forest

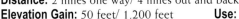

Distance: 2 miles one way/ 4 miles out and back
Elevation Gain: 50 feet/ 1,200 feet   **Use:** Light
Foot Difficulty: Moderate   **Biking Difficulty:** Difficult

Trail Location: access 1 East out of Grand Junction on I-70 to Exit #49. Turn right (S) on State Hwy 65 for 31 miles and turn right (SW) onto Lands End Road. Follow Lands End for 2.8 miles and make a left (SE) onto Carson Lake Road. Follow this road and park next to Carson Lake. Farmer's is 1.4 miles along Coal Creek just below the parking area and to the west.
access 2 Located 6 miles along the Kannah Creek. See Kannah Creek trail description on page 206.

East

Mileage Estimate (starting from access 1)
0.0-1.7m   Turn left (S) from Coal Creek junction along the badly eroded section and downhill steeply through the aspens.

1.7-2.0m   Wade in and out of Kannah Creek to the Kannah Creek junction and the end of the trail.

2.0-4.0m   Head back or continue along Kannah Creek or Spring Camp.

Trail Description: Farmer's slants steeply between Kannah Creek and Coal Creek Trails. It is marked in a few places, but if you are traveling uphill from the bottom, it is very hard to navigate your way along the correct trail due to all the cattle traffic ruts. It makes a good loop with Coal Creek, Kannah Creek and Carson Hole.

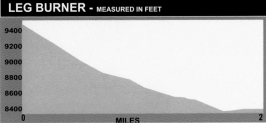

LEG BURNER - MEASURED IN FEET

9400
9200
9000
8800
8600
8400
0   MILES   2

Greenwood #721 - Grand Mesa National Forest

Distance: 3 miles one way/ 6 miles out and back
Elevation Gain: 325 feet/ 525 feet   **Use:** Moderate
Foot Difficulty: Easy-Moderate   **Biking Difficulty:** Moderate

Trail Location: East out of Grand Junction on I-70 to Exit #49. Turn right (S) on State Hwy 65 for 31 miles and turn right (SW) onto Lands End Road. Follow Lands End for 1 mile and make a left (SE) onto Flowing Park Road. Continue on Flowing Park for 3.5 miles and turn left (E) onto 1K Road. Park at the Bull and Brown Trailhead a half mile up the road.

East

Mileage Estimate

0.0-1.8m   This DT trail moves gently up and down through the trees and open meadows.

1.8-3.0m   The trail becomes very rocky and works its way up and down to the Granby Reservoirs. The trail ends at Granby Road/FR 115.

3.0-6.0m   Head back or follow Granby Road to Island Lake.

Trail Description: Greenwood is sandwiched between two ridges of the Mesa, one below and one above. It has an abundance of ideal fishing and camping spots as it goes through Granby Reservoirs, an area with at least 11 reservoirs in close proximity to each other. It also has an abundance of motorized traffic.

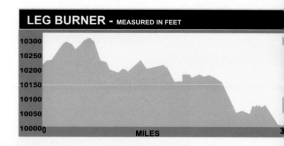

LEG BURNER - MEASURED IN FEET

10300
10250
10200
10150
10100
10050
10000
0   MILES   3

Indian Point Cutoff #708 - Grand Mesa National Forest

Distance: 2.2 miles one way/ 4.4 miles out and back
Elevation Gain: 650 feet
Use: Moderate
Foot Difficulty: Moderate
Biking Difficulty: Moderate

Trail Location: South out of Grand Junction 12 miles on U.S. Hwy 50 through Whitewater to Kannah Creek Road. Turn left (E) and follow the road 2.9 miles. Turn right (SE) and make another quick right (S). Then drive 6.2 miles to Kannah Creek/Spring Camp Parking Area. Indian Point Trail Cutoff is 4 miles along Spring Camp.

East

Trail Description: Indian Point Cutoff connects Spring Camp with Indian Point. Going the 1.8 miles to the top of the Mesa will take you to the Indian Point rock formations.

Mileage Estimate

0.0-2.2m Follow this steep trail up through the trees and meadows to the gate and the Indian Point junction.

2.2-4.4m Turn around here or continue this trail southeast another 1.8 miles along Indian Point to the top of the Mesa.

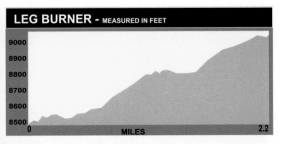

LEG BURNER - MEASURED IN FEET

Indian Point #715 - Grand Mesa National Forest

Distance: 11 miles one way/ 22 miles out and back
Elevation Gain: 200 feet/ 3,100 feet   **Use:** Moderate
Foot Difficulty: Moderate-Difficult   **Biking Difficulty:** Difficult

Trail Location: East out of Grand Junction on I-70 to Exit #49. Turn right (S) on State Hwy 65 for 31 miles and turn right (SW) onto Lands End Road. Follow Lands End for 1 mile and turn left (SE) onto Flowing Park Road. Continue Flowing Park for 5.5 miles and park at the Flowing Park Reservoir. Go southwest up through the gate.

East

Mileage Estimate

0.0-1.6m Follow the DT trail along the top of the Mesa to Chambers Reservoirs.

1.6-6.0m The trail turns right (SW) off the DT and across the alpine grassland. Go west to the edge of the Mesa and the Indian Point rock formations.

6.0-7.8m Follow the trail through the rocky switchbacks and to Indian Point Cutoff junction.

7.8-11.0m Continue left (W) and downhill along the western slope of the Mesa where the trail ends at the National Forest border.

11.0-22m Head back to your car.

Trail Description: Indian Point is a long trail, with a significant elevation change along the western slope of the Mesa. The trail offers breathtaking views of the Grand Valley and the unusual Indian Point rock formations from which the trail got its name.

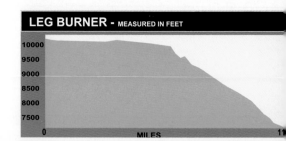

LEG BURNER - MEASURED IN FEET

10000
9500
9000
8500
8000
7500

0   MILES   11

Kannah Creek #706 - Grand Mesa National Forest

Distance: 8.8 miles one way/ 17.6 miles out and back
Elevation Gain: 4,150 feet   **Use:** Moderate
Foot Difficulty: Moderate   **Biking Difficulty:** Difficult

Trail Location: South out of Grand Junction 12 miles on U.S. Hwy 50 through Whitewater to Kannah Creek Road. Turn left (E) and follow the road 2.9 miles. Turn right (SE) and make another quick right (S). Then drive 6.2 miles to Kannah Creek/Spring Camp Parking Area and Kannah Creek trailhead.

East

Trail Description: Kannah Creek trail follows along the Kannah Creek through the adobe desert landscape to the alpine and ends at Carson Lake. It has an elevation change of 3,700 feet in 8.8 miles and is continuously rocky and steep on the way back.

Mileage Estimate

0.0-0.2m From the parking area, climb the hill to the Spring Camp junction.

0.2-5.9m Veer left (E) and cross several creeks on the way up a steep rocky hill to the upper Spring Camp junction.

5.9-8.8m Continue on the difficult trail uphill past Farmer's to Carson Lake.

8.8-17.6m Turn around and begin the wild trek back down.

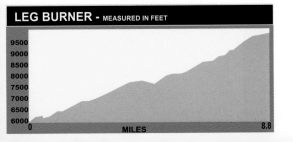

LEG BURNER - MEASURED IN FEET

MILES

Point Camp #725 - Grand Mesa National Forest

Distance: 3 miles one way/ 6 miles out and back
Elevation Gain: 700 feet
Foot Difficulty: Easy-Moderate   **Use:** Light
                                             Biking Difficulty: Moderate

Trail Location: South from Grand Junction on U.S. Hwy 50 to Delta. After reaching Delta, turn left (E) on State Hwy 92. Follow 92 and turn left (NE) onto State Hwy 65. Head north to Eckert to a left (W) onto 19.75 Road, and drive 15 miles. Park here.

East

Trail Description: Point Camp has many creeks to climb over and incredible views of the San Juan Mountains, Cedaredge and Delta. Along the way, there is the abandoned cabin pictured above.

Mileage Estimate

0.0-1.5m The trail works its way up through a few creeks and many fallen trees to an open meadow.

1.5-3.0m Follow the trail across the open grassland, through a few more creeks and climb out onto Cow Camp Road next to the Porter Reservoirs.

3.0-6.0m Head back or continue up Drop Off.

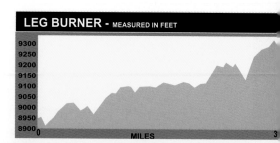

LEG BURNER - MEASURED IN FEET

9300
9250
9200
9150
9100
9050
9000
8950
8900

0   MILES   3

Spring Camp # 707 - Grand Mesa National Forest

Distance: 8 miles one way/ 16 miles out and back
Elevation Gain: 3,000 feet   **Use:** Moderate
Foot Difficulty: Moderate-Difficult   **Biking Difficulty:** Difficult

Trail Location: South out of Grand Junction 12 miles on U.S. Hwy 50 through Whitewater to Kannah Creek Road. Turn left (E) and follow the Kannah Creek road 2.9 miles. Turn right (SE) and make another quick right (S). Then drive 6.2 miles to Kannah Creek/Spring Camp Parking Area and Kannah Creek trailhead. Spring Camp begins east up the hill.

East

Mileage Estimate

0.0-2.5m Turn right (SE) at Kannah Creek junction and climb up the ridge through the trees and the oak brush.

2.5-4.0m The trail becomes more gentle as it reaches Indian Point Cutoff junction.

4.0-4.5m Stay straight through the aspens and across the creek to Blue Lake.

4.5-8.0m The trail becomes more difficult to follow because the signs are few and far between. Make your way downhill and across a few creeks to the Upper Kannah Creek junction.

8.0-16.0m Head back or make a loop with Kannah Creek.

Trail Description: Spring Camp climbs aggressively on a rocky ST for the first half then makes its way back downhill. Make the short hike up to Blue Lake if you can find the trail. It goes up through the junipers, the oak brush and the aspens and has amazing views of the Grand Valley.

LEG BURNER - MEASURED IN FEET

8500
8000
7500
7000
6500

0   MILES   8

Switchback #705 - Grand Mesa National Forest

Distance: 1.1 miles one way/ 2.2 miles out and back
Elevation Gain: 10 feet/ 750 feet   **Use:** Moderate
Foot Difficulty: Moderate-Difficult

Trail Location: access 1 12 miles south out of Grand Junction on U.S. Hwy 50 to
Kannah Creek Road. Turn left (E) and follow the road for 2.9 miles. Stay straight as the
road becomes Lands End Road. Follow Lands End for over 18 miles to the top at the Lands
End Road Visitor Center. Switchback is 4 miles east past the Visitor Center.
access 2 East out of Grand Junction on I-70 to Exit #49. Turn right (S) on State Hwy 65
for 31 miles and turn right (SW) onto Lands End Road. Follow Lands End for 8 miles to
the Switchback Trailhead on the left (S).

East

Mileage Estimate

0.0-1.1m Start atop the Mesa, down the steep
rocky section along the switchbacks
to the Coal Creek junction.

1.1-2.2m Head back or continue along
Coal Creek.

Trail Description: Switchback
is a foot travel only trail with a
sudden 800 feet down then
back up the southwestern rim of
the Mesa. It has incredible
views of Kannah Creek Basin.
Both Coal Creek and Coal
Creek Basin can be accessed
along this trail.

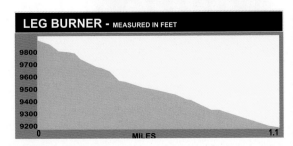

LEG BURNER - MEASURED IN FEET

9800	
9700	
9600	
9500	
9400	
9300	
9200	
0	MILES	1.1

South

The Uncompahgre Plateau is a step higher than the Grand Valley at 6,000 to 9,000 feet and is full of hidden-away trail systems along canyon bottoms, mesas and cottonwood-shaded creek beds. The Plateau, like the Grand Mesa, is a worthwhile escape during the summer for camping and sports. The deteriorating Dakota sandstone bluffs keep watch on the long distance Tabeguache Trail, which starts in Grand Junction and ends in Nucla: a trail as diverse as the Kokopelli Trail. The Plateau extends south past Unaweep and Dominguez Canyons to Escalante Creek that flows east to Delta from aspen groves down to pinyon and juniper woodlands. The Plateau is home to elk herds, mule deer, pronghorn antelope, burrowing owls, rare black bear, domesticated cattle and a healthy array of raptors. Explore the Plateau's trails and be assured of peaceful mid-week excursions in a cooler environment.

An edible treat or an emergency hydration food and medical source.
Virtually the entire plant is edible, it can be eaten raw or cooked—slice the pads lengthwise and scoop out the pulp. In late spring when the flower fades it leaves a fleshy fruit behind— good raw or made into a syrup. You can also split the pads to use as a compress on wounds.

Cactus Prickly Pear Nopal Opuntia
Basilaris

HWY 141

9280

South Lobe Creek

Spring

7380

West Bear

Gill Meadows

·2722

9320

Yellowjacket Canyon

North Fork

Middle Fork

Canyon

9020

P

9020

Corral Fork

8920

Fork

Little

7600

P

P

R 102 W

R 101 W

3

7

P

9250 Wolf Hill

Dead Horse Pasture

B 18 W

R 17 W

12

P

FR 405

FR 416

P

8300

Spring

8860

Massey

7490

Creek

Cow

Creek

FR 404

Creek

8070

p 215 Basin #603
p 216 Big Creek Scout #638
p 217 Big Creek & Cutoff #637
p 218 Cabin #606

p 219 Corral Fork #655
p 220 Gill Creek #602
p 221 Little Bear Lake #660
p 222 Little Creek #655

p 223 Middle
p 224 North F
p 225 Rim Tra
p 226 Snowsh

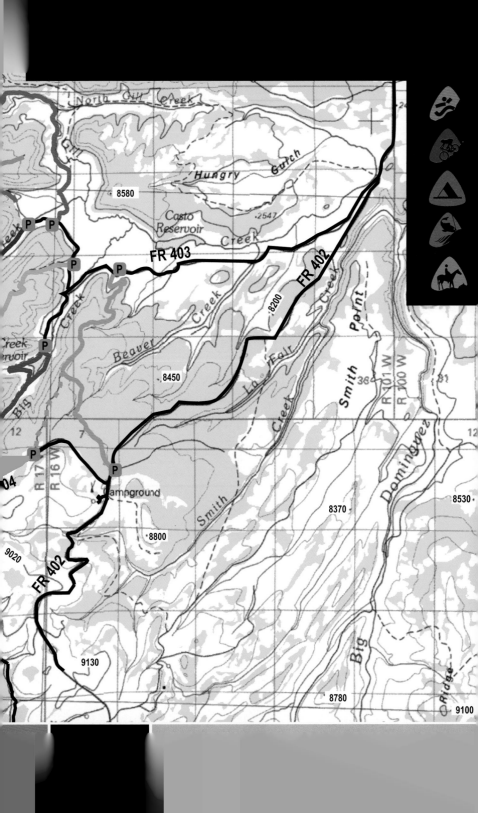

The Basin #603- Uncompahgre Plateau

Distance: 5.3 miles one way/ 10.6 miles out and back
Elevation Gain: 1,250 feet   **Use:** Moderate
Foot Difficulty: Easy-Moderate   **Biking Difficulty:** Moderate

Trail Location: 40 miles south out of Grand Junction on U.S. Hwy 50 to Whitewater. Turn right (SW) onto State Hwy 141. Follow it 14 miles up Unaweep Canyon and turn left (S) onto Divide Road/FR 402. Follow Divide Road for 10 miles and make a right (S) onto Big Creek Road/FR 403. Park at the Basin Trailhead 6 miles up Big Creek Road.

South

Mileage Estimate

0.0-2.5m   From where Big Creek Road ends, take the DT northwest and veer left at the Unaweep junction. Continue the moderate climb to Little Bear Lake on the right.

2.5-4.0m   Continue straight up to the Middle Fork junction through the pine forest.

4.0-5.3m   Continue straight to Rim Trail Road.

5.3-10.6m   Turn around or try Corral Fork, Snowshoe or North Fork.

Trail Description: The Basin Trail is a loose, rocky and sometimes sandy DT to the top of the plateau. Wildlife such as elk, deer, and even some domestic cows can be seen along the way to the spectacular views of the La Sal Mountains and canyons.

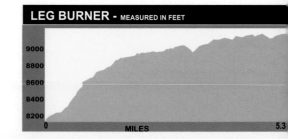

LEG BURNER - MEASURED IN FEET

Big Creek Scout # 638 - Uncompahgre Plateau

Distance: 3 miles one way/ 6 miles out and back
Elevation Gain: 850 feet   **Use:** Moderate
Foot Difficulty: Easy-Moderate   **Biking Difficulty:** Moderate-Difficult

Trail Location: 40 miles south out of Grand Junction on U.S. Hwy 50 to Whitewater. Turn right (SW) onto State Hwy 141. Follow it 14 miles up Unaweep Canyon and turn left (S) onto Divide Road/FR 402. Follow Divide Road for 10 miles and make a right (S) onto Big Creek Road/FR 403. Follow Big Creek Road for 4.6 miles and make a left (SW) before Cabin Trail. Follow this road for just under 1 mile to the base of Big Creek Reservoir. Park next to the dam.

South

Mileage Estimate

0.0-0.5m Go across the dam and follow the sandy DT to a gate and the Big Creek Scout sign.

0.5-0.8m As the DT goes left (SE), turn right (SW) and make your way across the creek that flows into the lake.

0.8-2.8m Follow this sometimes difficult and technical ST uphill on the right (NW) side of the creek to the tiny pond.

2.8-3.0m Turn left (SE) and go up to Uranium Road and the end of the trail.

3.0-6.0m Head back or continue on Rim and/or Big Creek Cutoff.

Trail Description: Big Creek Scout is an ST up through the wooded area to Big Creek Reservoir. Big Creek can be tough to cross in springtime when the water may be high due to snowmelt. Big Creek Reservoir and Big Creek are great places for fishing and camping.

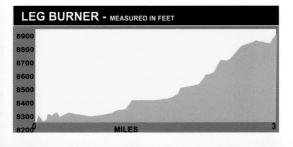

LEG BURNER - MEASURED IN FEET

8900
8800
8700
8600
8500
8400
8300
8200
0   MILES   3

Big Creek #656/Cutoff #637 - Uncompahgre Plateau

Distance: 3.6 miles one way/ 7.2 miles out and back
Elevation Gain: 900 feet   **Use:** Moderate
Foot Difficulty: Easy-Moderate   **Biking Difficulty:** Moderate

Trail Location: access 1 40 miles south out of Grand Junction on U.S. Hwy 50 to Whitewater. Turn right (SW) onto State Hwy 141. Follow it 14 miles up Unaweep Canyon and turn left (S) onto Divide Road/FR 402. Follow Divide Road for 10 miles and make a right (S) onto Big Creek Road/FR 403. Follow Big Creek Road for 3.9 miles and park here.
access 2 Follow Divide Road/FR 402 for 15.3 miles to just before Uranium Road. Park here on the right (W) side of Divide Road near the Divide Road/Uranium Road junction.

Mileage Estimate (starting from access 1)
0.0-1.6m Follow the rocky DT up a moderate climb to around 500 feet.

1.6-2.1m The trail levels off to the Big Creek Cutoff junction on the right (S).

2.1-3.6m Turn left (SE) at the Y intersection to Divide Road/FR 402.

3.6-7.2m Head back or loop with Big Creek Cutoff via Uranium Road.

Mileage Estimate (Big Creek Cutoff)
0.0-1.2m This trail is off Uranium Road and then downhill to the northeast through the trees to Big Creek. Follow Big Creek down to Casto Reservoir.

1.2-2.4m Turn around or continue on Big Creek, Scout or Cabin Trail.

Trail Description: Big Creek Cutoff is a fast way to get to Big Creek and Uranium Road and vice versa. It has an abundance of wildlife in the area, and offers splendid camping and fishing at Casto Reservoir at the end of Big Creek Cutoff.

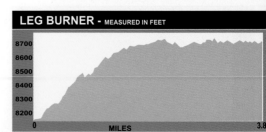

LEG BURNER - MEASURED IN FEET

8700
8600
8500
8400
8300
8200

0   MILES   3.8

Cabin Trail #606- Uncompahgre Plateau

Distance: 4 miles one way/ 8 miles out and back
Elevation Gain: 1250 feet   **Use:** Moderate
Foot Difficulty: Easy-Moderate   **Biking Difficulty:** Easy-Difficult

Trail Location: 40 miles south out of Grand Junction on U.S. Hwy 50 to Whitewater. Turn right (SW) onto State Hwy141. Follow it 14 miles up Unaweep Canyon and turn left (S) onto Divide Road/FR 402. Follow Divide Road for 10 miles and make a right (S) onto Big Creek Road/FR 403. Follow Big Creek Road for 5 miles and park here.

South

LEG BURNER - MEASURED IN FEET

9000
8900
8800
8700
8600
8500
8400
8300
8200
0   MILES   4

Mileage Estimate

0.0-1.5m Start from the cabin and go up a grueling 800 feet to an overlook.

1.5-3.5m The trail turns left (S) and goes down and back up to the Little Creek junction.

3.5-4.0m Continue uphill to Rim Trail Road.

4.0-8.0m Head back or continue on Rim Trail Road.

Trail Description: Cabin Trail is a very steep uphill at first, but then goes down to Rim Trail Road through the aspens and pines. At the top, get on the Rim Trail Road and take it to the Snowshoe, Basin, Middle Fork, or North Fork trails. Along the trail, an arm of Big Creek is visible.

Corral Fork #652 - Uncompahgre Plateau

Distance: 4.5 miles one way/ 9 miles out and back
Elevation Gain: 1,250 feet   **Use:** Moderate
Foot Difficulty: Moderate   **Biking Difficulty:** Moderate-Difficult

Trail Location: 40 miles south out of Grand Junction on U.S. Hwy 50 to Whitewater. Turn right (SW) onto State Hwy 141. Follow it 14 miles up Unaweep Canyon and turn left (S) onto Divide Road/FR 402. Follow Divide Road for 10 miles and make a right (S) onto Big Creek Road/FR 403. Park at the Corral Fork/Little Creek Trailhead 6 miles up Big Creek Road.

Mileage Estimate

0.0-1.0m At the end of Big Creek Road and at the start of Little Creek Trail, go uphill to the split in the trail.

1.0-4.5m Veer right (W) onto the section of the trail that becomes more technically and physically difficult. Go past a couple of fences and out to Rim Trail Road.

4.5-9.0m Head back or try Basin, Cabin, or Little Creek.

Trail Description: Corral Fork is a ST all the way up Little Creek and Corral Fork Creek through pine and aspen forest. The trail becomes more technically and physically difficult as it gets near the top. It makes a great loop with Cabin, Little Creek and Rim.

LEG BURNER - MEASURED IN FEET

9100	
9000	
8900	
8800	
8700	
8600	
8500	
8400	
8300	
8200	
8100	
	MILES 4.5

Distance: 5.7 miles one way/ 11.4 miles out and back
Elevation Gain: 400 feet/ 1,750 feet   **Use:** Moderate
Foot Difficulty: Moderate-Difficult   **Biking Difficulty:** Difficult

Trail Location: 38 miles south out of Grand Junction on U.S. Hwy 50 to Whitewater. Turn right (SW) onto State Hwy 141. Follow it 14 miles up Unaweep Canyon and turn left (S) onto Divide Road/FR 402. Follow Divide Road for 10 miles and make a right (S) onto Big Creek Road/FR 403. Follow Big Creek Road for 5.5 miles to the Gill Creek Trailhead and park on the right (N) side of the road.

South

Mileage Estimate

0.0-1.0m This trail begins north and downhill on a DT road through the gate to the creek.

1.0-2.1m Turn left (N) on the ST before the creek and follow it along the creek's left (W) side.

2.1-2.9m Cross the creek to the right (NE) on a DT. The trail narrows and plateaus along the ridge.

2.9-4.8m Drop steeply down over 1,200 feet into a canyon with lots of large rocks to navigate around. Be careful on your way down to the mouth of the canyon.

4.8-5.7m The trail exits the canyon to the right (NE) and levels off next to the private property. Continue to the dirt road next to Hwy 141.

5.7m-11.4m Turn around and climb up the 1,200 foot drop and back to the parking area.

Trail Description: Gill Creek is a DT/ST that travels along Gill Creek in the Uncompahgre National Forest, through a canyon to Hwy 141 and Unaweep Canyon. In the canyon, the trail becomes more physically challenging due to the elevation changes and the boulders you have to make your way around.

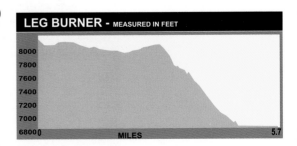

LEG BURNER - MEASURED IN FEET

8000
7800
7600
7400
7200
7000
6800

0   MILES   5.7

Little Bear Lake #660- Uncompahgre Plateau

Distance: 2.9 miles one way/ 5.8 miles out and back
Elevation Gain: 100 feet/ 350 feet   **Use:** Moderate
Foot Difficulty: Easy   **Biking Difficulty:** Easy

Trail Location: 40 miles south out of Grand Junction on U.S. Hwy 50 to Whitewater. Turn right (SW) onto State Hwy 141. Follow it 14 miles up Unaweep Canyon and turn left (S) onto Divide Road/FR 402. Follow Divide Road for 10 miles and make a right (S) onto Big Creek Road/FR 403. Park at the Basin Trailhead 6 miles up Big Creek Road. Little Bear Lake is 2.5 miles along Basin.

South

Mileage Estimate

0.0-2.9m Travel north from Basin junction along the level DT that then goes downhill along the ridge to the Gill Creek/Casto Reservoir overlook.

2.9-5.8m Head back and continue your journey along Basin, and Unaweep.

Trail Description: Little Bear Lake goes down a hill and along the short ridge. It is worth the trip to see the spectacular views of Gill Creek and Casto Reservoir. It goes across the Unaweep trail at the beginning after leaving the Basin trail.

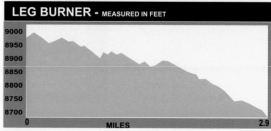

LEG BURNER - MEASURED IN FEET

Little Creek #655 - Uncompahgre Plateau

Distance: 3.5 one way/ 7.0 miles out and back
Elevation Gain: 1,060 feet   **Use:** Moderate
Foot Difficulty: Easy-Moderate   **Biking Difficulty:** Moderate-Difficult

Trail Location: 40 miles south out of Grand Junction on U.S. Hwy 50 to Whitewater. Turn right (SW) onto State Hwy 141. Follow it 14 miles up Unaweep Canyon and turn left (S) onto Divide Road/FR 402. Follow Divide Road for 10 miles and make a right (S) onto Big Creek Road/FR 403. Park at the Little Creek/Corral Fork Trailhead 6 miles up Big Creek Road.

South

Mileage Estimate

0.0-1.0m Follow the trail southwest uphill along Little Creek to where the trail splits.

1.0-1.5m Turn left (SW) and follow the trail across the creek and through the open grassland.

1.5-3.5m Follow the narrow ST uphill as it becomes more challenging through the canyon and the trees to where it meets Cabin junction.

3.5-7.0m Head back or continue along Cabin.

Trail Description: Little Creek is a really great ST trail that is technically challenging. The nearby Little Creek provides good fishing and camping spots. This trail is especially beautiful in the fall with the brilliant aspen colors.

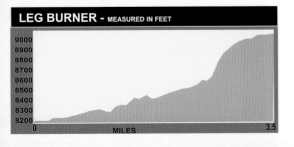

LEG BURNER - MEASURED IN FEET

9000
8900
8800
8700
8600
8500
8400
8300
8200
0   MILES   3.5

Middle Fork #654 - Uncompahgre Plateau

Distance: 1.5 miles one way/ 3 miles out and back
Elevation Gain: 970 feet   **Use:** Light
Foot Difficulty: Easy-Moderate   **Biking Difficulty:** Moderate

Trail Location: access 1 40 miles south out of Grand Junction on U.S. Hwy 50 to Whitewater. Turn right (SW) onto State Hwy 141. Follow it 14 miles up Unaweep Canyon and turn left (S) onto Divide Road/FR 402. Follow Divide Road for 15.4 miles and make a right (NW) onto Uranium Road. Follow Uranium Road for 2.8 miles and turn right (NW) onto Rim Trail Road. Follow Rim Trail for 4 miles and park at the Upper Basin Trailhead. Middle Fork starts 1.3 miles along Basin.

access 2 Middle Fork can also be accessed from the Unaweep Trail. Unaweep meets up with Middle Fork's base in Little Bear Canyon.

South

Mileage Estimate

0.0-1.5m Travel north off Basin on a narrow ST and quickly descends through the pine trees alongside the creek into Little Bear Canyon and to the Unaweep junction.

1.5-3.0m Head back or continue along the Unaweep trail or North Fork trail.

Trail Description: Middle Fork travels down through the pines and into Little Bear Canyon. It can make a pleasant loop with North Fork or a connector trail between Basin and Unaweep. It also has many wonderful camping sites and glimpses of wildlife.

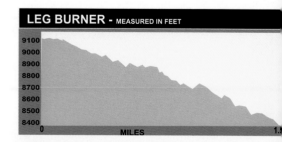

LEG BURNER - MEASURED IN FEET

MILES

North Fork #653 - Uncompahgre Plateau

Distance: 2.7 miles one way/5.4 miles out and back
Elevation Gain: 175 feet/ 1,100 feet   **Use:** Light
Foot Difficulty: Easy-Moderate   **Biking Difficulty:** Moderate

Trail Location:access 1 40 miles south out of Grand Junction on U.S. Hwy 50 to Whitewater. Turn right (SW) onto State Hwy 141. Follow it 14 miles up Unaweep Canyon and turn left (S) onto Divide Road/FR 402. Follow Divide Road for 15.4 miles and make a right (NW) onto Uranium Road. Follow Uranium Road for 2.8 miles and turn right (NW) onto Rim Trail Road. Follow Rim Trail for 5.2 miles and park at the trailhead. **access 2** North Fork can also be accessed from the Unaweep Trail. Unaweep meets up with North Fork's base in Little Bear Canyon.

South

LEG BURNER - MEASURED IN FEET

(Elevation profile ranging from 8300 to 9200 feet over 0 to 2.7 MILES)

Mileage Estimate

0.0-1.0m   Follow the trail northeast along the North Fork Creek to the canyon.

1.0-1.8m   Drop steeply into the canyon along the loose, rocky areas through an open meadow.

1.8-2.7m   Continue downhill to Unaweep junction and the end of the trail.

2.7-5.4m   Head back or continue along Unaweep in both directions.

Trail Description: North Fork is another way into Little Bear Canyon via a narrow creek side ST. It can be unstable in places but makes a great loop with Middle Fork. Every day, the elk drink out of the pond at the beginning of the trail.

The Rim #416- Uncompahgre Plateau

Distance: 5.5 miles one way/ 11 miles out and back
Elevation Gain: 850 feet   **Use:** Heavy
Foot Difficulty: Easy   **Biking Difficulty:** Easy-Moderate

Trail Location: 40 miles south out of Grand Junction on U.S. Hwy 50 to Whitewater. Turn right (SW) onto State Hwy 141. Follow it 14 miles up Unaweep Canyon and turn left (S) onto Divide Road/FR 402. Follow Divide Road for 15.4 miles and make a right (NW) onto Uranium Road. Follow Uranium Road for 2.8 miles and turn right (NW) onto Rim Trail Road. Park here.

South

Mileage Estimate

0.0-3.0m   Begin this trail to the northwest atop the plateau and along the fence.

3.0-3.5m   Turn left (W) after passing through the gate next to Cabin junction. Follow the more difficult DT to Basin junction on the right.

3.5-4.5m   Continue past Basin junction and then past Snowshoe junction over the rockiest section to Middle Pond.

4.5-5.2m   The trail weaves in and out along the road to the North Fork junction.

5.2-5.5m   Continue up to Far Pond and the overlook next to the radio antenna.

5.5-11.0m Head back or continue your journey on any of the other trails.

Trail Description: The Rim is an easy trek out to Far Pond and a lookout point with extraordinary views of the La Sal Mountains and the canyons of Gateway. At the end of the trail, there is an overlook of the canyons, the Grand Mesa National Forest/Fruita Lakes and the Unaweep trail. There can be heavy motorized traffic.

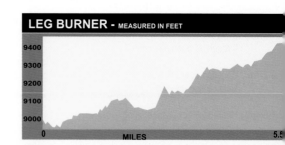

LEG BURNER - MEASURED IN FEET

9400
9300
9200
9100
9000

0   MILES   5.5

Snowshoe #607 - Uncompahgre Plateau

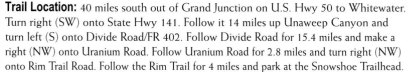

Distance: 1.25 miles one way/ 2.5 miles out and back
Elevation Gain: 20 feet/ 1,350 feet   **Use:** Light
Foot Difficulty: Difficult   **Biking Difficulty:** Extremely Difficult

Trail Location: 40 miles south out of Grand Junction on U.S. Hwy 50 to Whitewater. Turn right (SW) onto State Hwy 141. Follow it 14 miles up Unaweep Canyon and turn left (S) onto Divide Road/FR 402. Follow Divide Road for 15.4 miles and make a right (NW) onto Uranium Road. Follow Uranium Road for 2.8 miles and turn right (NW) onto Rim Trail Road. Follow the Rim Trail for 4 miles and park at the Snowshoe Trailhead.

South

Trail Description: Snowshoe starts off with a huge 1,300 foot drop off in 1.25 miles. This drop is loose and covered with rocks, making it difficult to trek up or down. It has incredible views of the La Sal Mountains in Utah to the west.

Mileage Estimate

0.0-0.5m	Carefully follow the downhill drop to Unaweep junction.
0.5-0.6	Turn right (W) then head to the Snowshoe junction.
0.6-1.25m	Turn left (SW) and go down the ST to the DT road.
1.25-2.5m	Turn around or make a monster loop by continuing the DT to Ute.

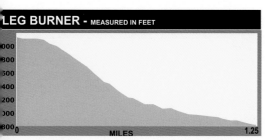

LEG BURNER - MEASURED IN FEET

1000
800
600
400
200
000
600
0   MILES   1.25

Unaweep #601 - Uncompahgre Plateau

Distance: 12.5 miles one way/ 25 miles out and back
Elevation Gain: 2,500 feet   **Use:** Moderate
Foot Difficulty: Moderate-Difficult

Trail Location: 40 miles south out of Grand Junction on U.S. Hwy 50 to Whitewater. Turn right (SW) onto State Hwy 141. Follow it 14 miles up Unaweep Canyon and turn left (S) onto Divide Road/FR 402. Follow Divide Road for 10 miles and make a right (S) onto Big Creek Road/FR 403. Park at the Basin Trailhead 6 miles up Big Creek Road. Unaweep Trail is less than half a mile along Basin Trail.

South

Mileage Estimate

0.0-0.3m Follow Basin to the Unaweep junction and turn right (N).

0.3-2.5m Follow the ST along a moderate climb through the trees to Little Bear Lake.

2.5-3.1m Turn right (NW) and cross over Little Bear Lake junction. Continue to an overlook.

3.1-5.0m Drop down the extremely steep narrow ST that makes its way to the base of Little Bear Canyon and Middle Fork junction. Turn right (N) to North Fork junction.

5.0-7.0m Continue north and make your way up and around to Yellow Jacket Canyon.

7.0-10.0m The trail goes up and down along the northern edge of the Uncompahgre National Forest.

10.0-12.5m The trail goes southeast and winds in and out of the mountain to Snowshoe junction and the end of the trail.

12.5-25.0m Head back or continue up the Snowshoe and travel Basin back down to the parking area.

Trail Description: Unaweep is a wild hike up, down, around and below the northern rim of the Uncompahgre National Forest. This trail is defined by drastic changes in elevation and rough rocky areas. It has the most beautiful views of the La Sal Mountains, and Western Colorado. There are short paths that branch off to overlook the Unaweep Canyon. Although this trail can be done as an out and back, it is easier to travel back to the parking area by way of Snowshoe and Basin.

LEG BURNER - MEASURED IN FEET

9100
9000
8900
8800
8700
8600
8500
8400
8300

MILES

Ute Creek #608- Uncompahgre Plateau

Distance: 7.7 miles one way/ 15.4 miles out and back
Elevation Gain: 830 feet/2,250 feet   **Use:** Moderate
Foot Difficulty: Moderate-Difficult   **Biking Difficulty:** Moderate-Difficult

Trail Location: access 1 45 miles from Grand Junction, take U.S. Hwy 50 south to Whitewater. Turn right (SW) on State Hwy 141. Follow it 14 miles up Unaweep Canyon and turn left (S) onto Divide Road/FR 402. Follow Divide Road for 15.4 miles and turn right (NW) onto Uranium Road. Follow Uranium Road for 3.4 miles and park at the Ute Creek Trailhead.
access 2 55 miles outside Grand Junction, take U.S. Hwy 50 south to Whitewater. Turn right (SW) onto State Hwy 141. Go 38 miles southwest and turn left (S) onto County Road 6.3. Follow this road for 2.7 miles along Pine Mountain and make a left/east on FR 607. Follow this road less than 2 miles and park at a corral and old barn.

South

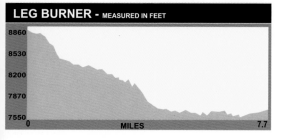

LEG BURNER - MEASURED IN FEET

8860
8530
8200
7870
7550
0   MILES   7.7

Mileage Estimate
0.0-2.9m From the top of the Uncompahgre Plateau, the trail travels steeply downhill along Indian Creek.

2.9-7.7m The trail turns left (NW) then northwest along the western slope of the Uncompahgre Plateau.

7.7-15.4m Climb back up or continue to the right (NE) to Snowshoe.

Trail Description: Ute Creek is a long trail that travels down along Indian Creek from atop the Uncompahgre Plateau. It becomes more primitive as it heads down and along the western slope of the Uncompahgre Plateau. Traveling along this route offers beautiful views of the La Sal Mountains and the western canyons around Gateway.

228

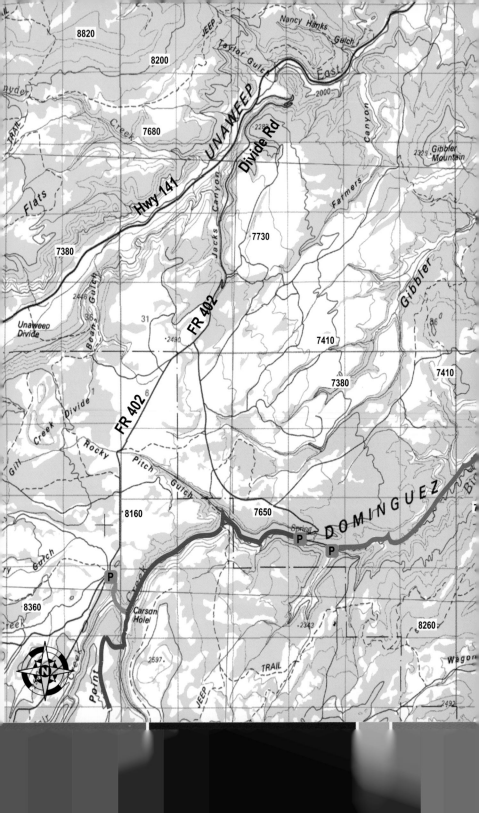

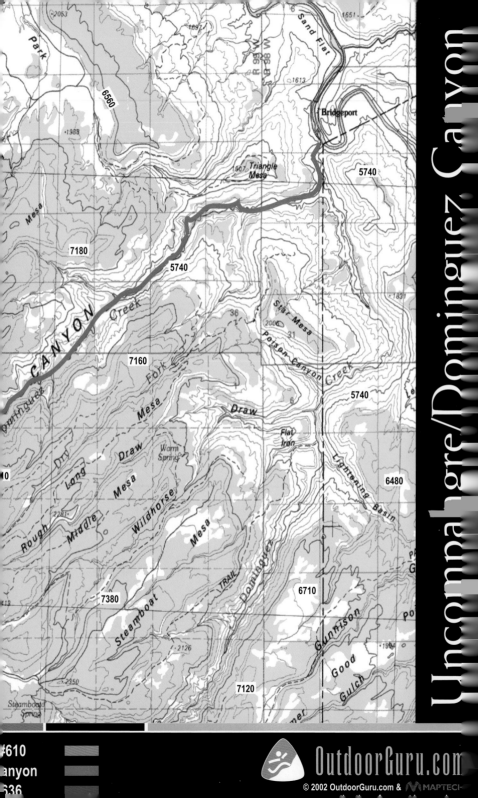

Bridgeport

5740

Triangle
Mesa

7180

5740

Star Mesa

Poison Canyon Creek

CANYON

Creek

7160

Fork

Mesa

Draw

5740

Dry

Long

Draw

Warm
Spring

Flat
Iron

Lightening Basin

6480

Rough

Middle

Mesa

Wildhorse

Mesa

Dominguez

TRAIL

6710

7380

Steamboat

Gunnison

Good

Gulch

7120

Steamboat
Spring

Park

6560

Sand Flat

Carson Hole #610 - Uncompahgre Plateau

Distance: 1.8 miles out and back
Elevation Gain: 50 feet/ 450 feet   **Use:** Heavy
Foot Difficulty: Moderate

Trail Location: 40 miles south out of Grand Junction on U.S. Hwy 50 to Whitewater. Turn right (SW) onto State Hwy 141. Follow it 14 miles up Unaweep Canyon and turn left (S) onto Divide Road/FR 402. Follow Divide Road for 10 miles just past Big Creek Road/FR 403 to the Carson Hole Picnic Grounds. Make a left/east, then a right (SE) at the Y in the road a short distance ahead. The Carson Hole Trailhead is a few hundred yards up from there.

South

Mileage Estimate

0.0-0.9m Follow this loose rocky trail as it plunges 400 feet from the canyon wall to the bottom of Carson Hole and the Smith Point junction.

0.9-1.8m Head back or continue either direction on Smith Point.

Trail Description: Carson Hole is a short, steep trail with the benefit of stunning views. Just as the name implies, it drops into a hole beneath the canyon walls. There are many places to camp in the area.

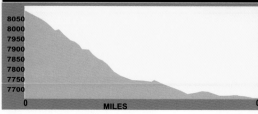

LEG BURNER - MEASURED IN FEET

8050	
8000	
7950	
7900	
7850	
7800	
7750	
7700	
0	0.9
	MILES

Dominguez Canyon - BLM (WSA)

Distance: 12.1 one way/ 24.2 miles out and back
Elevation Gain: 1500 feet/ 3,225 feet   **Use:** Light
Foot Difficult: Moderate-Difficult

Trail Location: 40 miles south out of Grand Junction on U.S. Hwy 50 to Whitewater. Turn right (SW) onto State Hwy 141. Follow it 14 miles up Unaweep Canyon and turn left (S) onto Divide Road/FR 402. Follow Divide Road for 6.1 miles to the Dominguez Canyon Recreation Area. Turn left (S) and then park at the Dominguez Canyon Trailhead 5 miles away.

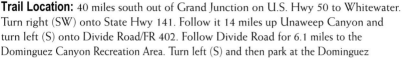

South

Mileage Estimate

0.0-4.2m The trail begins the long downhill descent along the Dominguez Creek.

4.2-7.2m Cross through a creek that comes from the north and continue downhill to the next creek crossing.

7.2-8.2m Continue the downhill descent along the beautiful rock walls through the canyon and meet up with the Lower Dominguez Canyon junction.

8.2-9.7m Turn left (E) at the Dominguez Canyon junction and follow the trail down along the sandstone walls.

9.7-10.2m Cross over the first creek and continue to the next creek crossing.

10.2-11.2m After crossing the second creek, the trail ends at the register box and the mapboard and where the creek and the Gunnison River come together.

11.2-22.4m Turn around and climb back up to the Dominguez Canyon Campground.

Trail Description: Dominguez Canyon is one of the most gorgeous canyons in this area. Waterfalls, unique sandstone rock formations, and developing arches all make this trail an ideal overnight trip. There are several places to camp out along this trail. Make sure you get to high ground if it rains, because the water will come rushing through the river and from atop the canyon like in the picture above. Bighorn sheep and other wildlife can be seen along the way. Dominguez Canyon is simply spectacular.

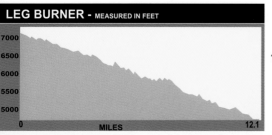

LEG BURNER - MEASURED IN FEET

7000	
6500	
6000	
5500	
5000	
0	MILES 12.1

Smith Point #636 - Uncompahgre Plateau/BLM

Distance: 7.0 miles one way/ 14 miles out and back
Elevation Gain: 1,600 feet/ 575 feet   **Use:** Moderate
Foot Difficulty: Easy-Moderate   **Biking Difficulty:** Moderate

Trail Location: access 1 40 miles south out of Grand Junction on U.S. Hwy 50 to Whitewater. Turn right (SW) onto State Hwy 141. Follow it 14 miles up Unaweep Canyon and turn left (S) onto Divide Road/FR 402. Follow Divide Road for 6.1 miles to the Dominguez Canyon Recreation Area. Turn left (S) and then park at the Smith Point Trailhead 4 miles away.
access 2 Located 0.7 miles at the end of Carson Hole.

South

Mileage Estimate

0.0-1.6m Follow the trail west along Dominguez Creek and the Dominguez Upper Canyon.

1.6-3.8m Turn left (S) and cross the creek and up the DT entering the Uncompahgre National Forest. Here the trail turns right (SW) along the ST on the right (W) hand side of Smith Creek. Pass Carson Hole junction to the next trail junction.

3.8-7.0m Turn right (W) and climb steeply to the top of Smith Point Ridge. The trail turns south along the top to the end of the trail and dirt road.

7.0-14m Head back to the parking area or try Carson Hole.

Trail Description: Smith Point travels southwest from BLM property along Dominguez Canyon and the Dominguez Creek with great fishing and camping spots. It has tremendous views of Dominguez Canyon as well as Carson Hole.

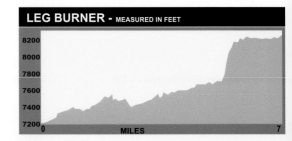

LEG BURNER - MEASURED IN FEET

(Elevation profile: y-axis from 7200 to 8200 feet, x-axis MILES from 0 to 7)

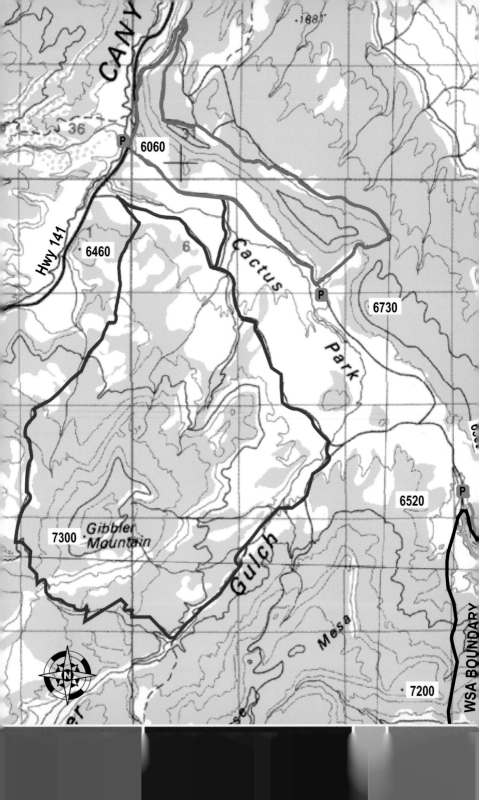

RIO GRANDE RIVER

Deer Run
4920
5520

WESTERN

Dad Flat

Tunnel Point

WSA BOUNDARY

5570

R 98 W
R 99 W

Sand Flat

5360

Bridge

Triangle Mesa

T 13 S
T 14 S

Ground

TRAIL

5740

21 Lower Dominguez
21 Triangle Mesa

Cactus Park Road Loop - Cactus Park

Distance: 8.4 mile loop
Elevation Gain: 1,650 feet
Foot Difficulty: Easy-Moderate

Use: Moderate
Biking Difficulty: Easy-Moderate

Trail Location: Just over 15 miles from Grand Junction. Travel south out of Grand Junction on U.S. Hwy 50 to Whitewater. Turn right (W) on State Hwy 141and go up Unaweep Canyon for 8 miles to the Cactus Park sign. Make a left (SE) and park at the cattle guard.

Mileage Estimate

0.0-2.3m Follow the main road southeast and stay straight (SE) until the Tabeguache junction.

2.3-3.1m Turn left (NE) begin a short and steep climb to the ridge on the rocky DT.

3.1-4.5m The trail drops a short distance and begins to turn left (N). Continue straight up the gentle climb to the DT junction.

4.5-5.7m Follow the DT and stay straight (NW) at 5.2 and 5.4 miles and continue to an overlook of Unaweep Canyon.

5.7-6.7m The trail veers left (N) and drops downhill toward the radio towers. Just before the towers is the next junction.

6.7-7.9m Make a hard left (SW) off Tabeguache and descend this steep rocky trail to Highway 141.

7.9-8.4m Merge right (SW) onto the highway and make a left (SE) into Cactus Park and back to the car.

Trail Description: Cactus Park Road Loop is along a portion of the main road into Cactus Park along the western base of the mountain ridge, before it heads up the ridge on the Tabeguache into the pinyon and juniper trees. There are awesome views atop the ridge of the Grand Valley, the Grand Mesa, and Unaweep Canyon.

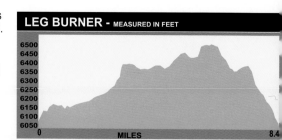

237

Dad's Flat - Cactus Park

Distance: 6.2 miles one way / 12.4 miles out and back
Elevation Gain: 750 feet/ 1,500 feet   **Use:** Moderate
Foot Difficulty: Easy-Moderate   **Biking Difficulty:** Moderate

Trail Location: Cactus Park is located 16 miles southwest of Grand Junction on U.S. Hwy 50 to Whitewater. Turn right (SW) onto State Hwy 141 8 miles up Unaweep Canyon to the Cactus Park sign. Make a left (E) onto the dirt road and follow it for 4 miles and make another left (E) onto a dirt road. Follow it 0.75 miles to where the DT turns to the right (S).

Mileage Estimate

0.0-1.4m Begin to the south along the rocky DT to where the trail moves east. There are great views from here to Triangle Mesa into a beautiful canyon.

1.4-2.0m The trail begins a downhill descent and to the north to a small canyon.

2.0-3.5m Drop into the small canyon and through the creek and climb back out northwest along the trail.

Trail Description: Dad's Flat is a good rocky DT that has awe inspiring views of nearby canyons, the Gunnison Bluffs, and the Grand Mesa. There are several chances to see some bighorn sheep like those pictured above. There are some steep declines and inclines along the way, and perhaps some ATV traffic.

3.5-6.2m The trail climbs to the west to the top of a ridge and then turns to the northeast goes downhill to the end of the trail overlooking the Gunnison Bluffs.

6.2-12.4m Turn around here and begin the climb back to Cactus Park and where you parked.

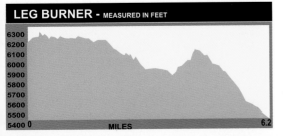

LEG BURNER - MEASURED IN FEET

6300
6200
6100
6000
5900
5800
5700
5600
5500
5400 0   MILES   6.2

Gibbler Mountain Loop - Cactus Park (WSA)

Distance: 15.3 mile loop
Elevation Gain: 1,650 feet
Foot Difficulty: Easy-Moderate

Use: Moderate
Biking Difficulty: Moderate

Trail Location: 15 miles south out of Grand Junction on U.S. Hwy 50 to Whitewater. Turn right (W) on State Hwy 141 and drive up Unaweep Canyon for 8 miles to the Cactus Park sign. Turn left (SE) and park at the cattle guard.

South

Trail Description: Gibbler Mountain Loop is a DT trail around Gibbler Mountain through the pinyon and juniper trees and through Gibbler Gulch. The trail is a mixture of sand, rocks, and slickrock.

Mileage Estimate

0.0-1.0m Travel up the road to the second right.

1.0-1.7m Turn right (S) and continue through a wash to the next junction.

1.7-2.9m Turn right (W) and follow this DT straight to the next junction.

2.9-5.2m Make a hard left (SE) and climb moderately up the DT over the sand and rock and stay straight (SW) at the 4.9 mile mark.

5.2-6.6m Veer left (S) at the slickrock area and back atop the DT trail to the next junction.

6.6-7.2m Make another hard left (E) and follow the loose rocky DT up to the top elevation at over 7,050 feet. If you miss this hard left, you won't go far because there is a fence just past the turn.

7.2-9.1m Drop quickly to the south until reaching the bottom of the wash and trail junction.

9.1-10.9m Now in Gibbler Gulch, turn left (NE) and twist, turn, and work out of the gulch back to the Tabeguache DT road.

10.9-11.3m Make a left (N) onto the Tabeguache Trail and continue to the next junction.

11.3-13.6m Turn left (N) at the Y intersection and another quick left (NW) and continue downhill to the next junction.

13.6-14.3 Turn right (N) onto the road, down through a wash and back to the main road.

14.3-15.3m Turn left (W) at the main road and follow it back to the car.

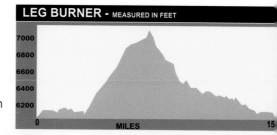

LEG BURNER - MEASURED IN FEET

7000
6800
6600
6400
6200

0   MILES   15

Lower Dominguez Canyon - Cactus Park (WSA)

Distance: 7 miles one way/ 14 miles out and back
Elevation Gain: 1,100 feet/2,300 feet   **Use:** Moderate
Foot Difficulty: Moderate-Difficult

Trail Location: Cactus Park is located 16 miles southwest of Grand Junction on US Route 50 to Whitewater. Turn right (SW) onto State Hwy 141 8 miles up Unaweep Canyon to the Cactus Park sign. Make a left (E) onto the dirt road and follow the road for 4 miles and make another left (E) on to a dirt road. Follow it 0.75 miles and park. Lower Dominguez begins here.

South

6.0-7.0m After crossing the second creek, the trail ends at the register box and the mapboard where the creek and the Gunnison River come together.

7.0-14.0m Turn around and head back.

Mileage Estimate

0.0-2.2m Begin this trail 2 miles from the Lower Dominguez sign and follow the DT to a steep uphill and back down past Triangle Mesa Road and the Lower Dominguez sign.

2.2-2.7m Turn right (SW) at the sign and follow the ST across the canyon ridge. Keep looking for the cairns to the left (S) for the drop off point.

2.7-3.0m Make a left (SE) and go down the loose dirt and slickrock of the canyon wall. Use extreme caution here.

3.0-5.5m Turn left (E) at the Dominguez Canyon junction and follow the trail down along the sandstone walls.

5.5-6.0m Cross over the first creek and continue to the next creek crossing.

Trail Description: Lower Dominguez Canyon is a great version of the long Dominguez Canyon Trail, described on page 232. It has amazing views atop Cactus Park and some rock features of Dominguez Canyon. Don't be surprised to see some bighorn sheep along the way. Keep in mind that a flood of water will come down the canyon after a rainfall, as seen in the picture to the left.

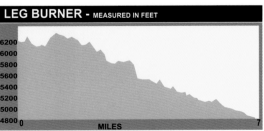

LEG BURNER - MEASURED IN FEET

6200
6000
5800
5600
5400
5200
5000
4800

0   MILES   7

Triangle Mesa - Cactus Park (WSA)

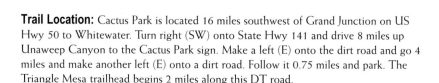

Distance: 4.8 mile loop
Elevation Gain: 1,200 feet   **Use:** Moderate
Foot Difficulty: Moderate

Trail Location: Cactus Park is located 16 miles southwest of Grand Junction on US Hwy 50 to Whitewater. Turn right (SW) onto State Hwy 141 and drive 8 miles up Unaweep Canyon to the Cactus Park sign. Make a left (E) onto the dirt road and go 4 miles and make another left (E) onto a dirt road. Follow it 0.75 miles and park. The Triangle Mesa trailhead begins 2 miles along this DT road.

Mileage Estimate

0.0-1.4m This hiking only trail crosses over a fence and down a very rocky DT along the northern wall of the canyon. It makes its way to the large Triangle Mesa in the distance.

1.4-3.4m Veer left (E) at the beginning of this loop, and travel around the north side of the Triangle Mesa. Along the way, the trail overlooks the Gunnison River and the north side of Dominguez Canyon.

3.4-4.8m Veer left (W) where you meet up with the loop again. Trek back up to the start of the loop.

Trail Description: Triangle Mesa loops around the unusual rock formation bearing the same name, and provides stunning views of the Gunnison River and Dominguez Canyon. This loose and rocky DT is for hiking only and has camping sites in Dominguez Canyon and Cactus Park.

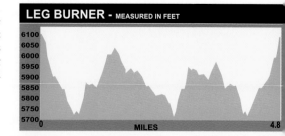

LEG BURNER - MEASURED IN FEET

6100
6050
6000
5950
5900
5850
5800
5750
5700
0   MILES   4.8

St. Mary's Hospital

The Regional Medical Center

- Cardiac Care Center
- Comprehensive Oncology Care
- Orthopedics
- Level II Trauma with Pediatric Commitment
- Psychiatric Services & Addiction Treatment

All Departments: 244-2273

To contact a patient directly:
dial 248-3 (and the room number)

BLOOD DONOR CENTER
2530 North 8th Street 244-2555

DIALYSIS CENTER
710 Wellington Avenue 244-7106

FAMILY PRACTICE CENTER
1160 Patterson Road.....................................244-2800

LIFE CENTER
1100 Patterson Road.....................................244-6100

ROSE HILL HOSPITALITY HOUSE
605 26 ½ Road..243-7968

St. Mary's CareFlight

Helicopter & Fixed Wing
Medical Transport
800-332-4923

Physicians, emergency medical services, law enforcement, and search and rescue personnel call 1-800-332-4923 to request CareFlight service, immediate care and rapid transport.

When every second counts.

RESPIRATORY CARE

Optimize to maximize!

St. Mary's Hospital offers **VO2 Max testing** to measure your oxygen consumption and aerobic fitness. Use these personal scores to optimize your exercise and nutrition program and maximize your athletic performance.

Call 970/244-2344 *to make an appointment with our Respiratory Care Department.*

"We're here for life."

(970) 244-2273

2635 N. 7th Street • P. O. Box 1628 • Grand Junction, CO 81502-1628
An Affiliate of the Sisters of Charity of Leavenworth Health System

McCarty Pack - Escalante Canyon (WSA)

Distance: 12.5 miles one way/ 25 miles out and back
Elevation Gain: 3,000 + feet   **Use:** Moderate
Foot Difficulty: Moderate   **Biking Difficulty:** Moderate-Difficult

Trail Location: Travel south out of Grand Junction on U.S. Hwy 50 for 27 miles and turn left (SW) at the Escalante Canyon access. Follow the road over the Gunnison River for 4.9 miles to the trailhead on the left (W) and park.

South

Mileage Estimate

0.0-1.8m From the parking area the trail begins west and at the most difficult spot climbs up a rocky DT then changes to a ST as the trail becomes steeper and goes up and around the McCarty Bench.

1.8-12.5m Here the trail makes a more gentle yet lengthy climb to the southwest along the top of Camp Ridge to Y5.00 Road and the end of the trail.

12.5-25.0m Turn around to complete the long out and back.

Trail Description: McCarty Pack is a DT/ST trail that heads quickly up the McCarty Bench and continues through the pinyons and junipers atop Camp Ridge. It has magnificent views of the Grand Mesa and the Gunnison River to where it ends just before the Uncompahgre National Forest.

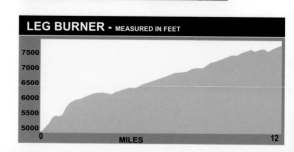

LEG BURNER - MEASURED IN FEET

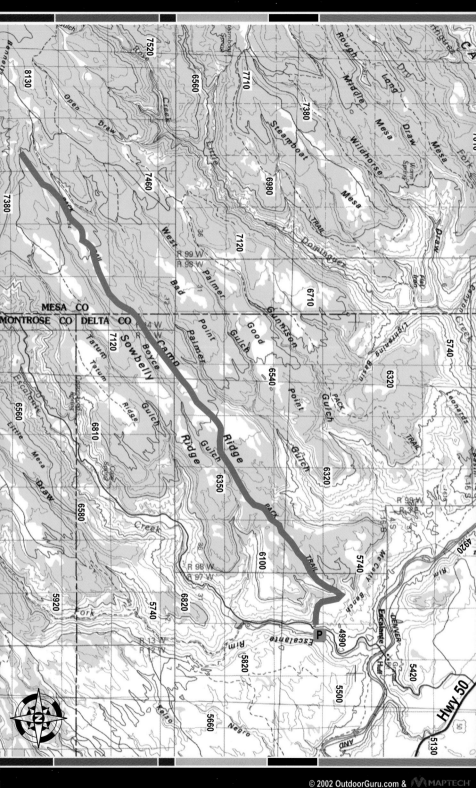

Campsite or Campground

The wild country of Western Colorado offers outdoor enthusiasts several options for making their outdoor adventures just the way they want them. This includes many organized campgrounds, or several areas where you can pick your own campsite. If you are planning to pick a campsite outside of an organized campground, please make sure you call the land management association in charge of the area you are going to and get all the regulations for campsites and especially campfires. These main numbers are available on page 16.

National Park Campgrounds–970.858.3617

SADDLEHORN CAMPGROUND
Located in the Colorado National Monument. Saddlehorn is at an elevation of 5,800 feet. There is a 14 day limit. There are very few RV sites and no hook ups. There is drinking water, but no dumping site or showers. There are 80 units and it costs $10 per night plus Colorado National Monument entrance fees This campground is wheelchair accessible.

Grand Mesa/Uncompahgre National Forest Campgrounds–970.856.4153

COBBETT LAKE(CARP LAKE)
This campground in the Grand Mesa National Forest is at an elevation of 10,300 feet, and has a 14 day limit. There are RV sites, with a maximum length of 30 feet and no hookups. There are 20 units and drinking water. There is not a dump site, or showers. The cost is $10 and this campground is not wheelchair accessible.

COTTONWOOD LAKE
This campground in the Grand Mesa is at an elevation of 10,000 feet. There is a 14 day limit, and RV sites have a maximum length of 30 feet. There are no hookups for any of the 42 units. There is drinking water, but not a dump site or showers. The cost is $10 and it is not wheelchair accessible.

CRAG CREST
This campground in the Grand Mesa is at an elevation of 10,100 feet. There is a 14 day limit on camping and a 30 foot length limit on RVs. There are no hookups for the 11 units. There is drinking water, but not a dump site or showers. The cost is $10 and it is not wheelchair accessible.

EGGLESTON
Located in the Grand Mesa, Eggleston is a group site at an elevation of 10,100 feet. There is a 14 day camp limit and reservations are required. RV sites with a maximum of 30 feet are available, but there are no hookups. This one unit can accommodate 30 people, and provides drinking water. There is no dump site or showers. The cost is $60 and is not wheelchair accessible.

ISLAND LAKE
This campground in the Grand Mesa is at an elevation of 10,300 feet. There is a 14 day limit, and a 45 foot limit for RVs. There are no hookups for the 41 units. There is drinking water, but not a dump site or showers. The cost is $10 and this campground is wheelchair accessible.

JUMBO
Located in the Grand Mesa, it is at an elevation of 9,800 feet. There is a 14 day limit, and a 22 foot length limit on RVs. There are no hookups at the 26 units. There is drinking water, but not a dump site or showers. The cost is $12 and it is not wheelchair accessible.

Kiser Creek

Located in the Grand Mesa at an elevation of 10,100 feet. There is a 14 day limit for camping. The RV sites have a 16 foot maximum length. There are no hookups for the 12 units. Drinking water is not available, nor is there a dump site or showers. The cost is $10 and it is not wheelchair accessible.

Little Bear

This campground is found in the Grand Mesa, at an elevation of 10,200 feet. It has a 14 day time limit, and a 22 foot maximum length on RVs. There are no hookups for the 36 units, but there is drinking water. There is no dump site, and no showers. The cost is $10 and it is wheelchair accessible.

Spruce Grove

Located in Grand Mesa, it is at an elevation of 9,900 feet. There is a 14 day limit, and a 22 foot limit on RVs. There are no hookups for any of the 16 units. There is drinking water, but not a dump site or showers. The cost is $10 and it is not wheelchair accessible.

Twin Lake

Located in the Grand Mesa, it is has an elevation of 10,300 feet. There is a 14 day limit, and a 22 foot limit on RVs. There are no hookups for the 13 units. There is no drinking water, nor a dump site or showers. The cost is $8 and it is not wheelchair accessible.

Ward Lake

This campground in the Grand Mesa is at an elevation of 10,200 feet. There is a 14 day limit on camping, and a 20 foot limit on RVs. There are no hookups for the 27 units. There is drinking water, but not a dump site or showers. The cost $12 and it is not wheelchair accessible.

Wier & Johnson

This campground in the Grand Mesa is at an elevation of 8,500 feet. There is a 14 day camping limit, and RVs are not allowed. There are no hookups at the 11 units. There is no drinking water, nor a dump site or showers. The cost is $8 and it is not wheelchair accessible.

Divide Forks

This campground is at an elevation of 8,700 feet. There is a 14 day limit, and RVs are not allowed. There are no hookups for the 10 units, but there is drinking water. There is not a dump site or showers. The cost is $8 and it is not wheelchair accessible.

Haypress

Located at 9,000 feet. There is a 14 day limit, and RVs are not allowed. There are no hookups available for the 11 units. There is also not drinking water, a dump site, or showers. There is no cost and it is not wheelchair accessible.

Bureau of Land Management Campgrounds–970.244.3000

Mud Springs

This campground is located at 7,000 feet, and has a 14 day camping limit. There is also a length limit of 30 feet for RVs. There are no hookups for the 12 units. There is drinking water, but no dump site or showers. The cost is $5 and it is wheelchair accessible.

Dominguez

This campground is at an elevation of 7,500 feet and has a 14 day camping limit. There are no RV units or hookups. There are only 9 units, and there is no drinking water, nor a dump site or showers. It doesn't cost anything, and it is not wheelchair accessible.

Rabbit Valley

This campground is located at an elevation of 4,500 feet. It has a 14 day time limit, and a 30 foot length limit on RVs. There are no hookups for the 8 units, and no drinking water. There is no dump site or showers. It doesn't cost anything, and it is not wheelchair accessible.

Colorado State Park Campgrounds–1-800-678-2267

HIGHLINE

Highline is at an elevation of 4,700 feet. It has a 14 day time limit, and reservations are required. The RVs have a length limit of 35 feet. There are no hookups for any of the 26 units. There is drinking water, a dump site, and showers. The cost is $9 plus the entrance fee for Highline State Park. This campground is wheelchair accessible.

ISLAND ACRES

This campground is at an elevation of 4,700 feet. It has a 14 day time limit, and reservations are required. The length limit on RVs is 75 feet. There are electric and full hookups for the 80 units. There is drinking water, a dump site, and showers. The cost can be $10, $14, or $16 plus the entrance fee to Island Acres State Park. This campground is also wheelchair accessible.

VEGA

This campground is at an elevation of 8,000 feet. There is a 14 day time limit, and reservations are required. The length limit for RVs is 40 feet and there are electrical and water hookups. There are 99 units. Drinking water, a dump site and showers are all available. The showers, however, are coin operated. The cost is $10 or $14 plus the entrance fee to Vega State Recreation Area. This campground is wheelchair accessible.

FRUITA

This campground is at an elevation of 4,500 feet. There is a 14 day time limit, and reservations are required. The RV length limit is 75 feet. There are electric and water hookups for the 63 units. There is drinking water, a dump site, and coin operated showers. The cost is $10, $14, or $16 plus the entrance fee. This campground is wheelchair accessible.

Campsites

You can camp anywhere you like in the Grand Mesa National Forest, the Uncompahgre Plateau, the Book Cliffs, and Cactus Park. Before setting out, contact the land management agency in charge of the area you are interested in and find out what restrictions may apply. Remember to ask if campfires are allowed.

Camping Etiquette

🌿 Check with the local ranger for suitable camping areas

🌿 Avoid areas that need to recover from overuse

🌿 Out of respect for other campers, keep the noise level down

🌿 Use an existing campsite whenever possible

🌿 If necessary to choose a new site, select one on sandy terrain or the forest floor instead of meadows, stream banks or other areas that will be scarred by a fire

🌿 Seek out a secluded area, it will increase privacy for you & others

🌿 Arrange tents to avoid concentrating activities in the cooking area

🌿 Avoid trenching around tents, cutting live branches, or pulling up plants

🌿 If you do move items in the area, like pine cones, scatter them back over the site

🌿 Leave the area as you found it, or in better condition

Fishing/Lakes and Rivers

Cool, crystal water flowing past you on all sides, or lapping against the shore at your feet illicits a calm, peaceful, one with nature feeling that only fishing seems to provide. Whether your preferred method is fly fishing or fishing from solid ground, Grand Junction and surrounding areas offer many fantastic places to fish. For several of these places, there are wonderful trails leading to them or near them. During the first full weekend of June of each year, you can enjoy these Colorado fishing spots without a license. So grab your fishing pole and bait and enjoy a hike or ride along a great trail and stop at a beautiful lake nearby.

Ice Fishing

Ice fishing is allowed on all bodies of water, unless specifically prohibited. Some places require the fishing shelter be temporary, while others allow permanent shelters. Contact the Colorado Division of Wildlife or the authority in charge of the area you want to ice fish to find out which kind of shelter is allowed.

Fly Fishing

Fly fishing provides the opportunity to get up close and personal with not only the fish, but Mother Nature as well. The Gunnison River, Colorado River, and several rivers and streams atop the Mesa provide excellent fly fishing spots. Many local fly fishers like to find the holding ponds along these smaller bodies of water, where the water pools. These holding ponds are especially great places to find bass and blue gill.

Lakes

There are a large number of exquisite lakes in Mesa and Delta County. By far the largest number of lakes in a particular area is the Grand Mesa. Several of these Grand Mesa lakes are favorites for local anglers, such as Lake Alexander, Island Lake, and Mesa Lake. And if a popular lake isn't what you're looking for, there are also a lot of the lesser known lakes, like McCurry Reservoir along the Battlement Trail, Deep Creek Reservoir #2 along Deep Creek Cutoff, Cold Sore Reservoir along Cottonwood, or Matt Arch Slough along Cobbett To Ward. We've gathered all the information we could about the 2002 restrictions on the lakes near the trails we've included in this guide. If a lake in this guide is not listed here then the state regulations apply. For a complete list of restrictions in Mesa and Delta County, check with the Colorado Division of Wildlife or pick up a copy of the most recent Colorado Fishing Season Information.

Some of the regulations dictate what kind of bait can be used. The Division of Wildlife defines artificial flies and lures as anything made of wood, plastic, glass, hair, metal, feathers or fiber that are made to catch fish. It does not include moldable material that attracts fish by taste or smell, or foods, such as worms, grubs, crickets, leeches, minnows, and fish eggs. The other area of regulation is in the size and amount, or bag and possession of fish that can be caught in a particular area. We have also provided general information, such as how popular the fishing location is, and what kind of fish can be caught. Fishing pressure refers to how much fishing is done at a particular lake, or how popular it is. Heavy fishing pressure might mean the chances of getting a bite are lower, if the lake is not stocked often. So when you are deciding where to cast that fishing line next, these are a few of the things you may take into consideration.

Big and Little Battlement Lakes

These lakes can be found at the end of the Battlement Trail. They have moderate fishing pressure, and are stocked annually with rainbow trout. The brook trout are from wild spawn.

Blue Lake

Blue Lake Trail leads to this lake that shares its name and has light fishing pressure. It is stocked annually with Colorado River and Snake River cutthroat trout. Boats and rafts are prohibited. Also, fishing along the shore is difficult here because it is covered with brush and boulders.

Bonham Reservoir
Bonham Reservoir can be accessed from the Bonham Trail and is another local favorite. That results in heavy fishing pressure on the cutthroat and creel sized rainbow trout in the lake. The information on how often these species are restocked was not available.

Bull Creek Reservoir #1, #2 and #5
Bull Creek #1 , #2 , and #5 are along Bull Creek Reservoir/Cutoff Trail. Bull Creek #1 and #2 have moderate fishing pressure and are stocked every other year with rainbow trout. Both of them only allow artificial lures or flies and the bag/possession and size limit is 2 fish, 16 inches or longer. Bull Creek #5 has light fishing pressure and carries rainbow and cutthroat trout.

Carson Lake
Carson Lake can be found along Deep Creek/Cutoff and the Carson Lake trails. It has moderate to heavy fishing pressure for the brook trout from wild spawn that swim here. Wading and all watercraft and boating is prohibited on this lake.

Cedar Mesa Reservoir
Cedar Mesa can be accessed from the Cedar Mesa Trail, and has moderate fishing pressure. The cutthroat trout found here are stocked every other year.

Cottonwood Reservoirs
Cottonwood Reservoirs can be found along the Lake of the Woods Trail. Cottonwood #4 has moderate fishing pressure on the rainbow trout stocked several times a year. Cottonwood #1 has heavy fishing pressure due in part to the variety of fish that can be found here. There is rainbow trout, cutthroat trout, brook trout, splake, and white suckers. The rainbow trout are stocked several times a year, the cutthroat and splake are stocked periodically, and the white suckers are from wild spawn. This lake also features a gravel boat ramp and easy access to the bank.

Deep Slough Reservoir
Deep Slough can be found along County Line and the Ward Creek trails. It has moderate fishing pressure and is stocked periodically with rainbow trout. White suckers can also be found in this lake.

Doughty Reservoir
Doughty Reservoir can be found along the Green Mountain Trail. It has moderate fishing pressure and rainbow and cutthroat trout. The rainbow are stocked periodically and the cutthroat are from wild spawn.

Eggleston Lake
Eggleston Lake can be accessed from the Crag Crest Trail. The fishing pressure is heavy and it is stocked several times a year with rainbow trout. White suckers can also be caught from this lake.

Forrest Lake
Forrest Lake can also be found along the Crag Crest Trail and has moderate fishing pressure. It has rainbow, brook and cutthroat trout. The cutthroat trout being stocked annually, the rainbow trout stocked periodically, and the brook trout occur from wild spawn only.

Granby Reservoirs
The Granby Reservoirs is an area of at least 8 lakes and can be reached at the end of Greenwood Trail. All of these lakes have moderate fishing pressure and are stocked every other year with rainbow trout. The only restriction is for Granby Reservoir #7, which does not allow motorized boats.

Griffith Lake

Griffith Lake can be found nearby the Lake of the Woods Trail, and has moderate fishing pressure. It is stocked annually with rainbow trout. This lake allows artificial flies or lures only, and the bag/possession, and size limit is 2 fish, 16 inches or longer.

Island Lake

Island Lake , naturally, can be found along the Island Lake Trail. Fishing pressure is heavy and it is stocked several times during the year with rainbow and brook trout, splake and white suckers. Ice fishing is the best way to catch the splake in this lake.

Knox Reservoir

Knox Reservoir can be found along Eureka /Eureka Cutoff trails, and has light fishing pressure. Neither the brook or cutthroat trout found here has been stocked in recent years.

Leon Lake

Leon Lake is found along Leon Lake Trail. It is a very large and popular fishing spot. It has moderate fishing pressure on the brook trout from wild spawn located here.

Lilly Lake

Lilly Lake can be found along Lilly Lake Trail, or a short distance from the East Lake of the Woods Trailhead Parking Lot. The fishing pressure is light at this naturally formed lake. The rainbow trout are stocked annually and the brook trout are from wild spawn.

Lost Lake

Lost Lake can be found along the Mesa Lakes to Lost Lake Trail, and has light fishing pressure. There are brook trout from wild spawn in this lake.

Mesa Lake

Mesa Lake is along Mesa Lakes to Lost Lake Trail, and also has heavy fishing pressure. It is stocked several times with the rainbow and brook trout available there.

Monument Reservoir #1

Monument Reservoir #1 is accessed from the Monument Trail and has light fishing pressure. The cutthroat trout found here are stocked every other year.

Porter Reservoirs

This group of reservoirs can be found near the end of the Point Camp and Dropoff trails. All of these lakes have moderate fishing pressure. The brook trout are stocked every other year.

Sunset Lake

Sunset Lake can be found along the West Bench Trail, and has heavy fishing pressure. It is stocked several times throughout the spring and summer and offers rainbow, brown and brook trout, as well as white suckers.

Vega Reservoir

Vega Reservoir can be found inside the Vega State Recreation Area. It has heavy fishing pressure in the summertime, and light to moderate fishing pressure in the winter. There are rainbow, cutthroat, brook, and brown trout as well as mottled sculpin. The rainbow trout are stocked annually, the cutthroat every other year, and the brook trout, brown trout, and mottled sculpin are from wild spawn.

Ward Lake

Ward Lake can be found along Ward Lake, or Cobbett to Ward trails. The fishing pressure is heavy with rainbow trout, brook trout, splake, and white suckers. The rainbow trout are stocked several times during the year, the splake are stocked periodically, and the brook trout and white suckers are from wild spawn.

Weir and Johnson Reservoir

Weir and Johnson Reservoir is accessed from the Leon Lake Trail. It has heavy fishing pressure because it is a very popular local fishing spot. The rainbow trout found here are stocked several times a year and the brook trout are from wild spawn.

Rivers and Creeks

The rivers and large creeks that flow through Western Colorado are suitable for traditional fishing as well as fly fishing. Several of them have trails that cross them many times, making that hunt for the perfect fishing spot a little bit easier.

Dirty George Creek

Dirty George is a 10.4 mile creek from the dam of Big Battlement Lake to Tongue Creek. In the last 6.7 miles, it passes through private property. It can be accessed from the Greenwood Trail or the Blue Grouse Trail. The fishing pressure for the brook and rainbow trout found here is not available. The best place to catch either of these kinds of fish is in that first mile below Big Battlement Lake.

Kannah Creek

Kannah Creek goes from Carson Lake to Flowing Lake Park Road. It can be accessed from Kannah Creek Trail, Coal Creek, Farmer's, or Coal Creek Basin trails. It has light-moderate fishing pressure, depending on which section of the river you are fishing. The farther away from the trailheads, the better chance there is of finding a place with light pressure. Above Carson Lake, there is just brook trout from wild spawn. Below Carson Lake, there is rainbow, brook, cutthroat and brown trout, all from wild spawn.

Ward Creek

Ward Creek travels 16.8 miles from Deep Slough Reservoir to Tongue Creek, with the lower 8.7 miles across private land. It can be accessed from Ward Creek or Ward Lake trails and has light to moderate fishing pressure. There is rainbow and cutthroat trout as well as white suckers. The cutthroat are stocked periodically. Beware of the steep sides and overgrown vegetation.

Fishing Resources

For more information on fishing any of the bodies of water in Mesa or Delta County, contact:

Colorado Division of Wildlife
303.297.1192/970.874.8616
www.wildlife.state.co.us

Delta Chamber of Commerce
www.deltacolorado.org

RECORDED INFORMATION
General Fishing Season Dates/Fees 303.291.7533
Fish Stocking Schedule 303.291.7531
Fishing Condition Report 303.291.7534

Colorado Fish in Danger

Fishing in Colorado can be fun for people of all ages and from all places. But Colorado's fish are a precious resource that must be taken care of, or they might be lost. Please help by releasing all fish you are not going to consume. One of the biggest problems the fish population faces is the spread of whirling disease. Whirling Disease is a parasitic infection that effects trout and salmon. It causes deformities, bizarre tail chasing spinning motions, and even death. You can't become infected with whirling disease by eating or handling an infected fish, it does not effect

humans. However, It has been linked to the drastic drop in native trout populations across the state. Although the disease has had very little effect on recreational fishing so far, it is important for the disease to be contained as much as possible. To help, please follow some simple steps every time you go fishing.

🐾 Wash off all mud from vehicles, boats, trailers, anchors, axles, fishing equipment, waders and boots

🐾 Drain boats, live bait wells, or any other container of water

🐾 Clean all equipment

🐾 Don't transport fish from one body of water to another, transporting fish without a license is illegal

🐾 Don't dispose of fish innards or any by products into any body of water

🐾 Never transport aquatic plants

🐾 Make sure boats, engine props, anchors, trailers and all wheels are free of weeds

Preparing for Your Outing

Whether biking, hiking, snowshoeing or strolling through the forest, you need to be prepared. Wear a comfortable outfit and have a reliable layering system and waterproof clothing for any sudden cold weather changes. It is also extremely important to take the right equipment on the outing. Do a double check before leaving, it is easy to forget something.

Make sure you pack useful items such as this guide, a topographic map, a compass, plenty of water for everyone, lots of nutritious food, matches, a knife, first aid kit, shelter, a cell phone and a global positioning unit. Be prepared for any mishaps like a bad spill off the bike, or a twisted ankle, or even hypothermia. In order to lessen your chances of encountering problems, make sure you know the environment you are heading into for the day. Elevation is a factor that must be considered, because it effects all trail users. Lightning is also a danger, so always check the weather forecast, and take cover if lightning is less then 5 miles away. If you are caught without shelter, crouch down on the balls of your feet, wrap your arms around your legs and cover your ears. Stay as low as possible and separated from others. If you do find shelter, wait until the storm has passed before leaving.

Wilderness Study Areas

Some of the areas covered in this trail guide are designated by Congress and the BLM as Wilderness Study Areas. An area is declared a WSA to determine if it should become a Wilderness Area after the study has been completed. During the study, the BLM takes responsibility to preserve the properties of the area that qualify it to be a WSA. In order to do this, human activities may be regulated if these activities pose a threat to the area. Of the areas this guide covers, there are two of them that are currently Wilderness Study Areas: Big Dominguez Canyon and the Little Book Cliffs. The Bureau of Land Management or other agency presiding over an area declared a Wilderness Study Area follows the guidelines set forth in the Wilderness Act of 1964. This act states:
"A wilderness, in contrast with those areas where man and his own works dominate the landscape, is hereby recognized as an area where the earth and its community of life are untrammeled by man, where man himself is a visitor and does not remain. An area of wilderness is further defined to mean in the Act an area of undeveloped Federal land retaining its primeval character and influence, permanent improvements or human habitation, which is protected and managed so as to preserve its natural conditions and which (1) generally appears to have been affected primarily by the forces of nature, with the imprint of man's work substantially unnoticeable; (2) has outstanding opportunities for solitude or a primitive and unconfined type of recreation; (3) has at least five thousand acres of land or is of sufficient size as to make practicable its preservation and use in an unimpaired condition; (4) may also contain ecological, geological, or other features of scientific, educational, scenic, or historical value."

Wilderness Area

There is one area covered by this guide that was a Wilderness Study Area and was declared a Wilderness Area. That area is the Black Ridge Canyons Wilderness, or the Colorado Canyons National Conservation Area (CCNCA). When a section of land is declared a Wilderness Area, the outdoor activities are limited to hiking and horseback riding only.

Contact #'s

Bureau of Land Management
970.244.3000

City of Grand Junction
970.244.1509

City of Palisade
970.464.5602

Colorado State Parks
Western Region Office
970.434.6862

Grand Mesa Visitor's Center
970.856.4153

Grand Mesa National Forest
970.874.7691

COPMOBA
www.copmoba.com

National Forest Foundation
202.501.2473

Leave No Trace
800.332.4100
www.LNT.org

The Wilderness Society
303.650.5818
www.wildernesssociety.com

Continental Divide Trail Alliance
303.838.3760

Sierra Club–Southwest Regional Office
303.449.5595
www.sierraclub.com

Keeping Notes of your excursion:

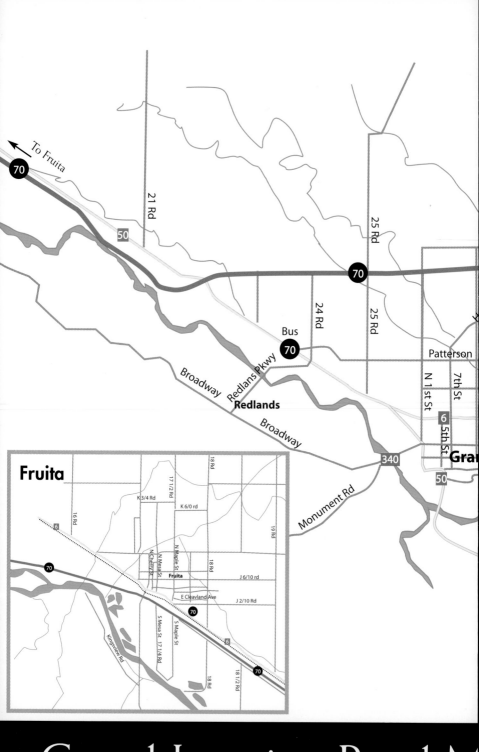

To Fruita

70

21 Rd

50

25 Rd

70

24 Rd

25 Rd

Bus
70

Patterson

N 1st St

7th St

Broadway

Redlans Pkwy

Redlands

6

5th St

Broadway

340

Gra

50

Monument Rd

Fruita

18 Rd

6

17 1/2 Rd

K 3/4 Rd

K 6/0 rd

16 Rd

19 Rd

70

N Cherry St

N Mesa St

N Maple St

18 Rd

Fruita

J 6/10 rd

E Cleavland Ave

J 2/10 Rd

6

70

Kingsview Rd

S Mesa St

S Maple St

17 1/4 Rd

18 Rd

18 1/2 Rd

70

Grand Junction Road M

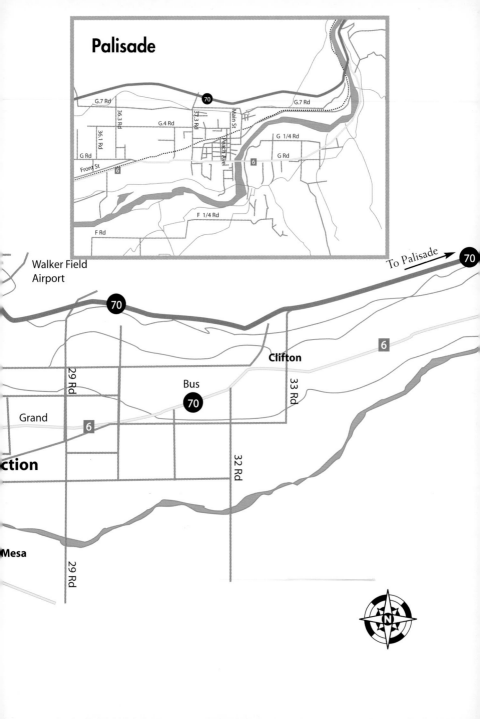

Thank you all for the memories and support.

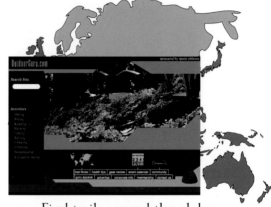
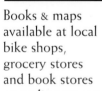